Clover Series

JN084374

English Booster!

Robert Hickling

Yasuhiro Ichikawa

KINSEIDO

Kinseido Publishing Co., Ltd.

3-21 Kanda Jimbo-cho, Chiyoda-ku,
Tokyo 101-0051, Japan

First published 2021 by Kinseido Publishing Co., Ltd.

Design　　　　Nampoosha Co., Ltd.
Illustrations　Tenki Takayama

Photos
p.16　© Ken Wolter|Dreamstime.com, © Ingus Kruklitis|Dreamstime.com,
　　　© Ken Wolter|Dreamstime.com;
p.17　© Jonathan Sim|Dreamstime.com;
p.28　© Toxawww|Dreamstime.com, © Maislam|Dreamstime.com;
p.34　© Pius Lee|Dreamstime.com;
p.35　© Andreistanescu|Dreamstime.com, © Djschreiber|Dreamstime.com;
p.40　© Bazruh|Dreamstime.com;
p.46　© Kharis Agustiar|Dreamstime.com;
p.70　© Bundit Minramun|Dreamstime.com;
p.71　© Jinyu1963|Dreamstime.com;
p.95　© Oliopi|Dreamstime.com, © Cowardlion|Dreamstime.com;
p.100 © Bukki88|Dreamstime.com

🎧 **音声ファイル無料ダウンロード**

https://www.kinsei-do.co.jp/download/4113

この教科書で 🎧 DL 00 の表示がある箇所の音声は、上記 URL または QR コードにて
無料でダウンロードできます。自習用音声としてご活用ください。

▶ PC からのダウンロードをお勧めします。スマートフォンなどでダウンロードされる場合は、
　ダウンロード前に「**解凍アプリ**」をインストールしてください。

▶ URL は **検索ボックスではなくアドレスバー (URL 表示欄)** に入力してください。

▶ お使いのネットワーク環境によってはダウンロードできない場合があります。

Ⓒ **CD 00**　左記の表示がある箇所の音声は、教室用 CD（Class Audio CD）に収録されています。

はじめに

English Booster! は英語を使う上で欠かせない必須文法を4技能を統合的に活用しながら学び、英語の基礎力をアップさせるテキストです。テーマ別に日常とビジネスの場面がバランスよく登場するストーリー仕立てとなっており、主人公である日本人大学生のカイがアメリカでホームステイとインターンシップを体験し、帰国後、就職活動を経て憧れの外資系IT企業に入社して自分の夢を叶えていくプロセスがユーモアたっぷりに描かれます。

1ユニットは6ページで構成され、全15ユニットから成ります。ユニットごとに特定の文法項目を取り上げており、またトピックに関連した語句が練習問題や例文も含めてユニットを通して使用されているので効果的な学習が可能です。さらに、TOEIC® L&Rテスト頻出語句が随所に使用されているのに加え、一部の問題形式もTOEIC L&Rテストを模していますので、やさしいレベルでの導入としてもお使いいただけます。

各ユニットの構成とおおよその時間の目安は次のようになっています。

Warm-Up Listening

ウォームアップとして、イラストを見ながら4つの短い文を聞いて最も適切なものを選ぶTOEIC Part 1形式の活動を行います。また、正解を確認したら実際にその文を書いてみます（5分）

Word Check

5つの英語の語句と日本語の意味をマッチングさせます。その後で、音声を聞いて発音を確認します（3分）

Kai's Blog

Word Checkの語句を使って短いブログを完成させます。その後で、音声を聞いて答えを確認します。このブログは次のConversationの導入になっています（7分）

Conversation

🅐 90〜130語程度の会話を聞いて4つのイラストを正しい順番に並べます（5分）

🅑 もう一度会話を聞いてTOEIC Part 3形式の質問に答えます（5分）

🅒 最後にもう一度会話を聞いて、ユニットの文法項目に関する会話中の空所を書き取ります。また、この会話を使ってスピーキングの練習をすることもできます（10分）

Grammar **Menu**

ユニットで取り上げた文法項目のポイントを、トピック関連語句を使用した例文とともに簡潔に説明してあります（15分）

Grammar **Checkup**

A 空所に入る正しい語句を選んで短い文を完成させるTOEIC Part 5形式の文法練習問題です（5分）

B 日本語の意味に合うように与えられた語句を並べ替えて文を完成させます（7〜8分）

C 空所に入る正しい語句を選んで2人の人物による短い会話を完成させます。その後で、音声を聞いて答えを確認します。また、この会話を使ってスピーキングの練習をすることもできます（7〜8分）

Good Reading

A トピックに関連する80〜100語程度の英文を読み、選択肢から正しい語句を選んでユニットの文法項目に関する文中の空所を埋めます。その後で、音声を聞いて答えを確認します（10分）

B もう一度英文を読んでTOEIC Part 7形式の質問に答えます（5分）

Writing—**About Me** ※Unit 2を除く

A 主人公のカイの答えを参考にしながら、自分の情報を記入して表を完成させます（7〜8分）

B **A**のカイの答えをもとに、与えられた語句を使ってユニットの文法項目に関する文中の空所を埋め、カイに関する短いパラグラフを完成させます（7〜8分）

C **B**を参考にして今度は自分について書いてみることで、学習した文法項目の理解とそれを用いて効果的に自分のことを書く力がついたかを確認します（10〜15分）

なお、巻末には各ユニットに登場した重要語句のリストがついていますので、予習や復習、または確認テストなどにお使いいただけます。

最後に、本書の制作にあたり、金星堂のみなさまから多くの助言、支援をいただきました。この場をお借りして御礼申し上げます。

著者

本書は CheckLink（チェックリンク）対応テキストです。

CheckLinkのアイコンが表示されている設問は、CheckLinkに対応しています。

CheckLinkを使用しなくても従来通りの授業ができますが、特色をご理解いただき、授業活性化のためにぜひご活用ください。

CheckLinkの特色について

大掛かりで複雑な従来のe-learningシステムとは異なり、CheckLinkのシステムは大きな特色として次の3点が挙げられます。

1. これまで行われてきた教科書を使った授業展開に大幅な変化を加えることなく、専門的な知識なしにデジタル学習環境を導入することができる。
2. PC教室やCALL教室といった最新の機器が導入された教室に限定されることなく、普通教室を使用した授業でもデジタル学習環境を導入することができる。
3. 授業中での使用に特化し、教師・学習者双方のモチベーション・集中力をアップさせ、授業自体を活性化することができる。

▶教科書を使用した授業に「デジタル学習環境」を導入できる

本システムでは、学習者は教科書のCheckLinkのアイコンが表示されている設問にPCやスマートフォン、アプリからインターネットを通して解答します。そして教師は、授業中にリアルタイムで解答結果を把握し、正解率などに応じて有効な解説を行うことができるようになっています。教科書自体は従来と何ら変わりはありません。解答の手段としてCheckLinkを使用しない場合でも、従来通りの教科書として使用して授業を行うことも、もちろん可能です。

▶教室環境を選ばない

従来の多機能なe-learning教材のように学習者側の画面に多くの機能を持たせることはせず、「解答する」ことに機能を特化しました。PCだけでなく、一部タブレット端末やスマートフォン、アプリからの解答も可能です。したがって、PC教室やCALL教室といった大掛かりな教室は必要としません。普通教室でもCheckLinkを用いた授業が可能です。教師はPCだけでなく、一部タブレット端末やスマートフォンからも解答結果の確認をすることができます。

▶授業を活性化するための支援システム

本システムは予習や復習のツールとしてではなく、授業中に活用されることで真価を発揮する仕組みになっています。CheckLinkというデジタル学習環境を通じ、教師と学習者双方が授業中に解答状況などの様々な情報を共有することで、学習者はやる気を持って解答し、教師は解答状況に応じて効果的な解説を行う、という好循環を生み出します。CheckLinkは、普段の授業をより活力のあるものへと変えていきます。

上記3つの大きな特色以外にも、掲示板などの授業中に活用できる機能を用意しています。従来通りの教科書としても使用はできますが、ぜひCheckLinkの機能をご理解いただき、普段の授業をより活性化されたものにしていくためにご活用ください。

CheckLink の使い方

CheckLink は、PC や一部のタブレット端末、スマートフォン、アプリを用いて、この教科書にある ↻CheckLink のアイコン表示のある設問に解答するシステムです。

・初めて CheckLink を使う場合、以下の要領で**「学習者登録」**と**「教科書登録」**を行います。

・一度登録を済ませれば、あとは毎回**「ログイン画面」**から入るだけです。CheckLink を使う教科書が増えたときだけ、改めて**「教科書登録」を行ってください。**

CheckLink URL

https://checklink.kinsei-do.co.jp/student/

登録は CheckLink 学習者用**アプリが便利です。ダウン**ロードはこちらから ▶ ▶ ▶

▶学習者登録 (PC /タブレット/スマートフォンの場合)

①上記 URL にアクセスすると、右のページが表示されます。学校名を入力し「ログイン画面へ」を選択してください。
PC の場合は「PC 用はこちら」を選択して PC 用ページを表示します。同様に学校名を入力し「ログイン画面へ」を選択してください。

②ログイン画面が表示されたら**「初めての方はこちら」**を選択し「学習者登録画面」に入ります。

③自分の学籍番号、氏名、メールアドレス（学校のメールなど **PC メールを推奨**）を入力し、次に**任意のパスワード**を8桁以上20桁未満（半角英数字）で入力します。なお、学籍番号はパスワードとして使用することはできません。

④「パスワード確認」は、❸で入力したパスワードと同じものを入力します。

⑤最後に「登録」ボタンを選択して登録は完了です。次回からは、「ログイン画面」から学籍番号とパスワードを入力してログインしてください。

▶教科書登録

①ログイン後、メニュー画面から「教科書登録」を選び（PCの場合はその後「新規登録」ボタンを選択）、「教科書登録」画面を開きます。

②教科書と受講する授業を登録します。
教科書の最終ページにある、**教科書固有番号**のシールをはがし、印字された**16桁の数字とアルファベット**を入力します。

③授業を担当される先生から連絡された**11桁の授業ID**を入力します。

④最後に「登録」ボタンを選択して登録は完了です。

⑤実際に使用する際は「教科書一覧」（PCの場合は「教科書選択画面」）の該当する教科書名を選択すると、「問題解答」の画面が表示されます。

▶問題解答

①問題は教科書を見ながら解答します。この教科書の ⟳CheckLink のアイコン表示のある設問に解答できます。

②問題が表示されたら選択肢を選びます。

③表示されている問題に解答した後、「解答」ボタンを選択すると解答が登録されます。

▶CheckLink 推奨環境

PC
推奨 OS
  Windows 7, 10 以降
  MacOS X 以降

推奨ブラウザ
  Internet Explorer 8.0 以上
  Firefox 40.0 以上
  Google Chrome 50 以上
  Safari

携帯電話・スマートフォン
  3G 以降の携帯電話（docomo, au, softbank）
  iPhone, iPad（iOS9 〜）
  Android OS スマートフォン、タブレット

・最新の推奨環境についてはウェブサイトをご確認ください。
・上記の推奨環境を満たしている場合でも、機種によってはご利用いただけない場合もあります。また、推奨環境は技術動向等により変更される場合があります。

▶CheckLink 開発
CheckLink は奥田裕司 福岡大学教授、正興 IT ソリューション株式会社、株式会社金星堂によって共同開発されました。

CheckLink は株式会社金星堂の登録商標です。

CheckLink の使い方に関するお問い合わせは…

正興ITソリューション株式会社　CheckLink 係

e-mail　checklink@seiko-denki.co.jp

English Booster!

Character Profiles

Kai

東京のCompTech大学でITを専攻する大学生
趣味はバスケットボールとCGアニメ制作
将来の夢はアプリのデザイナー
シリコンバレーでのインターンシップを兼ねて
ホームステイ先のサンフランシスコへ旅立つ

San Francisco

Wendy

(Unit 2, 5, 7, 9)
カイのホームステイ先の
ホストシスター

Brian
Wendyの弟

Mr. Nelson　**Mrs. Nelson**
Wendyの両親

Silicon Valley

Jack

(Unit 3)
インターンシップ先の
デザイン部長

Linda

(Unit 4, 6, 8, 11, 15)
インターンシップ先の
同僚

Tom

(Unit 4, 15)
インターンシップ先の
同僚

TechIzUs

Sam
(Unit 12)
日本にある外資系IT企業
TechIzUs 社の部長

Hana
(Unit 13, 14)
TechIzUs 社の同僚

Tina

On a plane

Cabin Attendant

(Unit 1)
カイがサンフランシスコへ
向かう飛行機の客室乗務員

Passenger

(Unit 10)
カイが帰国する飛行機で
同乗する女性

Unit 1

On My Way to Silicon Valley

Grammar	現在時制
Vocabulary	**Travel**

Warm-Up Listening

4つの英文を聞いてイラストに最も合っているものを選びましょう。その後で、正解の文を書いてみましょう。

CheckLink　DL 002　CD1-02

Ⓐ　Ⓑ　Ⓒ　Ⓓ　　Kai is _____.

Word Check

次の英語の意味に合う日本語を選びましょう。

CheckLink　DL 003　CD1-03

1. abroad　　　　（　　）
2. destination　　（　　）
3. flight　　　　（　　）
4. nervous　　　（　　）
5. polite　　　　（　　）

a. 目的地
b. 神経質な、緊張している
c. 海外に
d. ていねいな
e. 航空便、空の旅

Kai's Blog

上の Word Check の語句を使ってKaiのブログを完成させましょう。
その後で、音声を聞いて答えを確認しましょう。　DL 004　CD1-04

Right now, I'm on an airplane. My ¹_____ is San Francisco, California. This is my first time to travel ²_____, so I'm a little ³_____. The ⁴_____ is smooth, and the cabin attendants are very kind and ⁵_____, but sometimes I don't understand their English.

Conversation

A Kaiと客室乗務員の会話を聞いて順番に絵を並べましょう。

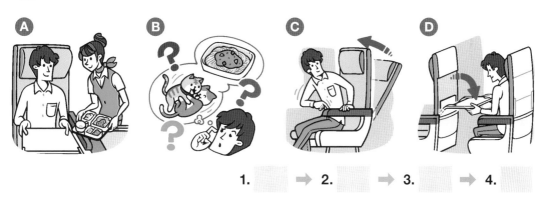

1. ⬜ ➡ 2. ⬜ ➡ 3. ⬜ ➡ 4. ⬜

B もう一度会話を聞いて質問に最も合う選択肢を選びましょう。

ᏟCheckLink   DL 005   CD1-05

1. What are Kai's lunch choices?

- Ⓐ Chicken or pasta
- Ⓑ A tuna sandwich or a salad
- Ⓒ *Tonkatsu* or pasta
- Ⓓ An omelet or a salad

2. What does the cabin attendant ask Kai to do?

- Ⓐ Adjust his seat
- Ⓑ Put on his seatbelt
- Ⓒ Return to his seat
- Ⓓ Put his tray table up

C もう一度会話を聞いて空所を埋めましょう。   DL 005   CD1-05

Cabin Attendant (CA): Sir, please ¹_____ your seat to the upright position.

Kai: Upright position?

CA: Yes, it's lunchtime. Your seat ²_____ to be straight up.

Kai: Oh, I'm sorry. … OK, there.

CA: Thank you. Do you ³_____ pasta or *katsu* for lunch?

Kai: Excuse me, pasta or what?

CA: *Katsu*. Umm … *tonkatsu*.

Kai: Oh, *tonkatsu*, not cats. You ⁴_____ … meow! Ha ha ha! … Whew! … Umm, pasta, please.

CA: All right. Please ⁵_____ your tray table down.

Kai: Oh, right. Sorry.

CA: That's, OK. … Here you are. ⁶_____ your meal.

Kai: Thank you.

Grammar Menu

現在時制は主に現在の次のようなことを表す場合に使われます。
　①意見や感情　②状態　③事実や真実とされること　④繰り返される動作

①意見・感情	Kai **wants** to join a package tour of San Francisco. (Kaiはサンフランシスコのパック旅行に参加したいです)
	The National Gallery **is** popular among tourists. (ナショナル・ギャラリーは観光客に人気です)
②状態	The hotel **is** full of Los Angeles Angels fans. (ホテルはロサンゼルス・エンゼルスのファンで満室です)
	The departure lobby of Terminal 2 **looks** busy. (第2ターミナルの出発ロビーは混んでいるようです)
③事実・真実	The Computer History Museum **closes** at 6 p.m. (コンピューター歴史博物館は6時に閉館します)
	Chicago **is** very cold in winter. (冬、シカゴはとても寒いです)
④繰り返される動作	A bus to the airport **comes** every twenty minutes. (空港へのバスは20分ごとに来ます)
	The Computer History Museum **opens** at 9 a.m. from Tuesday to Sunday. (コンピューター歴史博物館は火曜から日曜まで午前9時に開きます)

形　式

be動詞	肯定文	I **am** / You **are** / He/She/It **is**	a tourist/late.	
	否定文	I'm **not** / You **aren't** / He/She/It **isn't**		
	疑問文	**Am** I / **Are** you / **Is** he/she/it	a tourist/late**?**	
	肯定文	We/You/They **are**	tourists/late.	
	否定文	We/You/They **aren't**		
	疑問文	**Are** we/you/they	tourists/late**?**	
一般動詞	肯定文	I/You/We/They **travel**	a lot.	
	否定文	I/You/We/They **don't travel**		
	疑問文	**Do** I/you/we/they **travel**	a lot**?**	
	肯定文	He/She/It **travels**	a lot.	
	否定文	He/She/It **doesn't travel**		
	疑問文	**Does** he/she/it **travel**	a lot**?**	
be動詞	命令文	**Be**	quiet in the palace.	
	（否定）	**Don't be**	late for your flight!	
一般動詞	命令文	**Fasten**	your seat belt.	
	（否定）	**Don't forget**	your passport.	

動詞の-(e)sの付け方（語尾変化のパターン）

meet→meet**s**, stay→stay**s**	語尾にsを付ける
finish→finish**es**, teach→teach**es**	語尾がss/sh/ch/x/oの動詞にはesを付ける
try→tr**ies**, carry→carr**ies**	語尾が子音＋yの動詞はyをiesに変える
have→**has**, be→**is/am/are**	不規則な変化をする（特別な形）

Take Note
● Be動詞と一般動詞は続けて使うことはありません。（×I **am go** to Hawaii by ship.）
● 命令文には主語がなく、否定する場合はdon'tを付けます。

Grammar **Checkup**

A (　　) 内のa〜cから適当な語句を選んで文を完成させましょう。　CheckLink

1. Hawaii and Guam (**a.** is　**b.** are　**c.** do) popular with Japanese travelers.
2. (**a.** Are　**b.** Does　**c.** Do) you have your passport?
3. Tom and Jane always (**a.** travel　**b.** flies　**c.** trips) economy class.
4. Harry (**a.** doesn't likes　**b.** isn't like　**c.** doesn't like) group tours.
5. The tourists (**a.** come from　**b.** comes from　**c.** are come from) the U.S.
6. Please (**a.** don't　**b.** not　**c.** you don't) take pictures in the museum.

B 日本語を参考にして、語句を並べ替えて文を完成させましょう。
（文頭の語も小文字になっています）

1. your suitcase / help / you / with / need / do （スーツケースを運ぶ手伝いが必要ですか）

_____ ?

2. seafood / town / is / for / famous / this （この町はシーフードで有名です）

_____ .

3. you / stay / your / hope / we / enjoy （私たちはあなたが滞在を楽しむことを望みます）

_____ .

4. many / shops / airport / duty-free / the / has （その空港にはたくさんの免税店があります）

_____ .

C (　　) 内のa〜cから適当な語句を選んで会話を完成させましょう。その後で、音声を聞いて答えを確認しましょう。　CheckLink　DL 006 ~ 007　CD1-06 ~ CD1-07

1 *At a train station* （駅で）

A: Excuse me. [1](**a.** Does　**b.** Is　**c.** Do) this train go to Rose Station?

B: No, this [2](**a.** are　**b.** has　**c.** is) an express train. [3](**a.** It's not stop
  b. It doesn't stop　**c.** It's no stop) at Rose Station.

2 *At a hotel* （ホテルで）

A: Hi. I [1](**a.** am　**b.** do　**c.** have) a bad cold. [2](**a.** Are　**b.** Does　**c.** Is)
  there a clinic near the hotel?

B: Yes, here's a map. But please hurry—it [3](**a.** close　**b.** closes
  c. is close) at noon.

Good Reading

CheckLink   DL 008   CD1-08

A Silicon Valleyに関する文章を読んで、下のa〜cから適当な語句を選んで空所に書いてみましょう。その後で、音声を聞いて答えを確認しましょう。

Silicon Valley

Silicon Valley is in the San Francisco Bay Area in Northern California. It [1]_____ the city of San Jose. The Bay Area's other two major cities are San Francisco and Oakland. About eight million people [2]_____ in the Bay Area. Silicon Valley is home to many world-famous high-technology companies such as Facebook, Google and Yahoo!. Around 60% of people with high-tech jobs in the Bay Area [3]_____ in Silicon Valley. And students from around the world [4]_____ about high technology at one of the many excellent universities in and around Silicon Valley. Stanford University and the University of California, Berkeley are two examples.

1.	a. have	b. includes	c. makes
2.	a. live	b. living	c. lives
3.	a. business	b. job	c. work
4.	a. educate	b. learn	c. teach

B もう一度文章を読んで質問に最も合う選択肢を選びましょう。   CheckLink

1. Where is Silicon Valley?

Ⓐ In the city of San Francisco
Ⓑ In San Jose
Ⓒ In the state of California
Ⓓ In the city of Silicon

2. What is Silicon Valley famous for?

Ⓐ World-famous fashion brands
Ⓑ High-technology companies
Ⓒ Harvard University
Ⓓ Sports and entertainment

Writing—About Me

A Kaiの例を参考にして、自分の情報を書いてみましょう。

Name	Kai Suzuki	
Age	20	
Place of birth	Hamamatsu,Shizuoka Prefecture	
Name and location of university	CompTech University/ Tokyo	
Main area of study	information technology	
Free time activities	play basketball, create computer animation	

B 下の動詞を正しい形に変えて、Kaiに関する文章を完成させましょう。

attend   be   create   play   study

Kai Suzuki [1] _____ 20 years old. He's from Hamamatsu, Shizuoka Prefecture. He [2] _____ CompTech University in Tokyo. He [3] _____ information technology. He [4] _____ basketball and [5] _____ computer animation in his free time.

C **B** を参考にして、自分のことを書いてみましょう。

My name _____. _____ years old. I'm from _____

_____

_____

_____

Welcome to San Francisco

Grammar	代名詞
Vocabulary	Homestay English

Warm-Up Listening

4つの英文を聞いてイラストに最も合っているものを選びましょう。その後で、正解の文を書いてみましょう。　⟲CheckLink　🎧 DL 009　◎ CD1-09

San Francisco International

Ⓐ　Ⓑ　Ⓒ　Ⓓ　　Kai is _____.

Word Check

次の英語の意味に合う日本語を選びましょう。　⟲CheckLink　🎧 DL 010　◎ CD1-10

1. excited about （　　）
2. house rules （　　）
3. interests （　　）
4. look forward to （　　）
5. worry （　　）

a. 心配する
b. 興味、関心
c. 家の決まり
d. を楽しみにする
e. にワクワクする

Kai's Blog

上の Word Check の語句を使ってKaiのブログを完成させましょう。その後で、音声を聞いて答えを確認しましょう。　🎧 DL 011　◎ CD1-11

I'm ¹ _____ my homestay, and I ² _____ meeting Mrs. Nelson, my host mother. But I also ³ _____. Does everyone in my host family speak quickly? Are their ⁴ _____ all different from mine? Do they have a lot of ⁵ _____? Hmm …

A KaiとWendyの空港での会話を聞いて順番に絵を並べましょう。

A  **B**  **C**  **D**

1. ➡ 2. ➡ 3. ➡ 4.

B もう一度会話を聞いて質問に最も合う選択肢を選びましょう。

CheckLink DL 012 CD1-12

1. Who is Wendy?

- **A** Kai's homestay mother
- **B** Kai's roommate
- **C** Kai's classmate
- **D** Kai's homestay sister

2. Where is Mrs. Nelson?

- **A** At home
- **B** At work
- **C** In the airport
- **D** In the airport parking lot

C もう一度会話を聞いて空所を埋めましょう。 DL 012 CD1-12

Wendy: Excuse me. Is ¹_____ name Kai?

Kai: Yes, it is. Are you Mrs. Nelson?

Wendy: What? … No, sorry, my mom's still at her office. I'm Wendy Nelson, your homestay sister. Welcome to San Francisco.

Kai: Thank you very much.

Wendy: My brother and ²_____ are here to take you to ³_____ house. Brian's in the car in the parking lot. He hates airports. ⁴_____ always so crowded.

Kai: Well, this is my first trip abroad … and I think I hate ⁵_____, too.

Wendy: Ha ha ha! Yeah. … Well, I'm sure you're tired, Kai, so let's go home. Here, let me help ⁶_____ with your luggage.

代名詞には次のような特徴があります。

①すでに登場した名詞の代わりに使われ、代わりとなる名詞の人称や単数／複数によって形が
　異なる

②所有格は名詞の前に来る

③所有代名詞は名詞として使われる

④再帰代名詞はイディオム表現としてよく使われる

①名詞の代わり	This is Henry Johnson. **He** is the head teacher in this school. （こちらはヘンリー・ジョンソンさんです。彼はこの学校の主任教員です） There are about 20 foreign students in this college. **They** come from various countries. （この大学には約20名の留学生がいます。彼らはさまざまな国の出身です）
②所有格	This is Mrs. Nelson. She is **your** host mother. （こちらはネルソンさんです。彼女はあなたのホストマザーです） Kai is **our** homestay student from Japan. （カイは日本から来た私たちのホームステイの学生です）
③所有代名詞	This is your room, and that one is **mine**. （ここがあなたの部屋で、あそこが私の（部屋）です） Our customs are different from **theirs**. （私たちの習慣は彼らの（習慣）とは異なります）
④再帰代名詞	They enjoyed **themselves** at our welcome party. （彼らは私たちの歓迎パーティーで楽しみました） Please make **yourself** at home. （どうぞおくつろぎください） Kai introduced **himself** to his homestay family. （カイはホームステイ先の家族に自己紹介しました）

形　式					
	主格 （主語「～は」）	目的格 （目的語「～を」）	所有代名詞 （「～のもの」）	所有格 （「～の」）	再帰代名詞 （「～自身」）
単数	I	me	mine	my	myself
	you	you	yours	your	yourself
	he	him	his	his	himself
	she	her	hers	her	herself
	it	it	——	its	itself
複数	we	us	ours	our	ourselves
	you	you	yours	your	yourselves
	they	them	theirs	their	themselves

Take Note

● itにはさまざまな用法があります

時間：**It** is seven thirty. **It's** time to go to school. （7時30分です。学校へ行く時間です）

天候：**It** is very cold today. （今日はとても寒いです）

距離：**It** is two kilometers from here to school. （ここから学校まで2kmあります）

● Theyは「人」を示す「彼ら」だけでなく、「それら」という意味にもなります。

I have a lot of bags. **They** are all made in England.

（私はたくさんバッグを持っています。それらはすべてイギリス製です）

Grammar **Checkup**

A ( ) 内のa〜cから適当な語句を選んで文を完成させましょう。 ⟳CheckLink

1. Kai's host sister's name is Wendy. (a. Hers　b. She　c. Her) hobby is hiking.

2. This plate is hot.　Be careful not to burn (a. your　b. yours　c. yourself) fingers.

3. Mr. Nelson and (a. her　b. him　c. his) wife often host homestay students.

4. These pancakes are really light and fluffy.　I love (a. their　b. them　c. they).

5. Please give (a. I　b. me　c. my) the recipe for this dish.

6. The blue bath towel in the bathroom is (a. you　b. your　c. yours).

Note fluffy「ふわふわした」

B 日本語を参考にして、語句を並べ替えて文を完成させましょう。
（文頭の語も小文字になっています）

1. you / meet / happy / I'm / to / very　（私はあなたに会えてとてもうれしいです）

　_____.

2. I / understand / question / sorry, / your / don't　（すみません、私はあなたの質問がわかりません）

　_____.

3. a / gift / you / here's / small / for　（これはあなたへのささやかな贈り物です）

　_____.

4. meat / to / help / more / and vegetables / yourself
（どうぞご自由にもっと肉や野菜を食べてください）

　_____.

C ( ) 内のa〜cから適当な語句を選んで会話を完成させましょう。 その後で、音声
を聞いて答えを確認しましょう。 ⟳CheckLink 🎧DL 013 ~ 014 ◎CD1-13 ~ ◎CD1-14

1 *In the kitchen*（台所で）

A: Do [1](a. you　b. your　c. you're) like all vegetables?

B: Well, green peas aren't [2](a. me　b. my　c. mine) favorite vegetable.

A: How about carrots?

B: Actually, I don't really like [3](a. it　b. they　c. them), either.

2 *In the laundry room*（洗濯室で）

A: This is [1](a. our　b. us　c. ours) laundry room.　Please feel free to use
the washing machine anytime.

B: Is [2](a. it　b. its　c. they) difficult to use?

A: No, not at all. Here, let [3](a. I　b. mine　c. me) show you.

Good Reading

A インターンシップとホームステイに関する文章を読んで、1〜4の代名詞が表わしているものを下のa〜cから選びましょう。その後で、音声を聞いて答えを確認しましょう。

Internships and Homestays

Every year, hundreds of Japanese university students do internships in English-speaking countries. The students get new skills and business know-how. ¹ They also become better English speakers and learn about the host country and ² its people. Many students combine their internship with a homestay. Most of the host families have children, often the same age as the homestay students. Students enjoy talking with ³ their host family members at mealtime, and doing fun and interesting activities with ⁴ them at night and on weekends.

Notes combine「組み合わせる」 the same age as ...「…と同じ年齢の」

1. **a.** internships	**b.** English-speaking countries	**c.** students
2. **a.** host family's	**b.** host country's	**c.** student's
3. **a.** students'	**b.** family's	**c.** children's
4. **a.** children	**b.** students	**c.** host family members

B もう一度文章を読んで質問に最も合う選択肢を選びましょう。　CheckLink

1. What advantage of internships does the reading mention?

- **A** Meeting new people
- **B** Learning time management
- **C** Making money
- **D** Getting business know-how

2. What advantage of homestays does the reading NOT mention?

- **A** Safety
- **B** Speaking opportunities
- **C** Enjoying meals together
- **D** Doing weekend activities

Note mention「について述べる」

Writing—Character Profile

A Kaiの好きなアニメのキャラクターのプロフィールを参考にして、自分の好きなキャラクター、俳優、歌手、スポーツ選手の情報を書いてみましょう。

Name	Conan Edogawa	
Age	6 or 7	
Height & weight	95 cm / 18 kg	
Date of birth	May 4th	
Occupation	student, detective	
Nickname	Conan-kun	
Interests	soccer, karaoke	
Family	Yusaku Kudo (father), Yukiko Kudo (mother)	
Other	Parents hope son becomes a great detective.	

Note detective「探偵」

B 下の代名詞を使って、**A** のキャラクターに関する文章を完成させましょう（1回以上使うものもあります）。

> he   him   his   their   they

Conan Edogawa is 6 or 7 years old. ¹_____ is 95 cm tall and weighs 18 kg.
²_____ birthday is May 4th. ³_____ is a student and a detective.
⁴_____ nickname is Conan-kun. Conan-kun likes soccer and karaoke.
Everyone tells ⁵_____ that ⁶_____ is a terrible singer.
⁷_____ parents are Yusaku and Yukiko Kudo. ⁸_____ always push
⁹_____ son to become a great detective.

C **B** を参考にして、**A** で書いたキャラクターや人物について書いてみましょう。

_____

_____

_____

_____

_____

First Day of Internship

Grammar	前置詞（時・場所）
Vocabulary	**At a company**

Warm-Up Listening

4つの英文を聞いてイラストに最も合っているものを選びましょう。その後で、正解の文を書いてみましょう。　　CheckLink 🎧 DL 016 ◎ CD1-16

Ⓐ　Ⓑ　Ⓒ　Ⓓ　　Kai's _____.

Word Check

次の英語の意味に合う日本語を選びましょう。　　CheckLink 🎧 DL 017 ◎ CD1-17

1. first impressions （　　）
2. headquarters （　　）
3. shuttle bus （　　）
4. tight （　　）
5. uncomfortable （　　）

a. 気まずい、落ち着かない
b. 本社、本部
c. きつい、余裕がない
d. 往復バス
e. 第一印象

Kai's Blog

上の Word Check の語句を使ってKaiのブログを完成させましょう。その後で、音声を聞いて答えを確認しましょう。　🎧 DL 018 ◎ CD1-18

Today is the first day of my internship. I'm on a ¹_____ to the company ²_____ now. It's near my homestay family's house. It only takes about 15 minutes to get there. I'm ³_____ wearing a suit, and my tie feels ⁴_____ around my neck! But ⁵_____ are very important, I think.

CheckLink 🎧 DL 019 ◎ CD1-19

A Kaiとデザイン部門の部長Jackの会話を聞いて順番に絵を並べましょう。

A  **B**  **C**  **D**

1. ⬜ ➡ 2. ⬜ ➡ 3. ⬜ ➡ 4. ⬜

B もう一度会話を聞いて質問に最も合う選択肢を選びましょう。

CheckLink 🎧 DL 019 ◎ CD1-19

1. How long is the lunch break?

  A 40 minutes
  B 50 minutes
  C 60 minutes
  D 70 minutes

2. What does Jack ask Kai to wear every day?

  A His sneakers
  B A T-shirt
  C His ID badge
  D A tie

C もう一度会話を聞いて空所を埋めましょう。 🎧 DL 019 ◎ CD1-19

Jack: Our office hours are ^{1}_____ 9:00 ^{2}____ 5:00, with 50 minutes for lunch.

Kai: Are there any restaurants ^{3}_____ here?

Jack: Yes, there are several restaurants nearby. … Now, we have a business casual dress code here, Kai. Do you understand the meaning of that?

Kai: It isn't necessary to wear a suit and tie?

Jack: That's right. But please don't wear a T-shirt, jeans, sneakers or sandals.

Kai: I understand.

Jack: Oh, and thanks for your photo. Here's your ID badge. Always wear it ^{4}_____ office hours.

Kai: Instead of my tie?

Jack: Yes, leave your tie ^{5}_____ home. … Well, let me introduce you to some of the people ^{6}_____ the design department.

Note instead of … 「…の代わりに」

Grammar **Menu**

使い方のPOINT

前置詞は「時」や「場所」を表す場合に使われ、後ろには名詞（句）が続きます。

①時を表す前置詞
- 「年」「月」「季節」in
- 「曜日」「日付」「1日の一部」on
- 「時間」at / from / to / since / until / by / after / before / in
- 「時期・期間」for / during

②場所を表す前置詞
- 「位置」「目的地」at / on / in / off / out of / away / from
- 「通路」across / through / past
- 「経路を伴う移動」up / down / along / across / to / toward / from A to B / through
- 「相対的位置」above / below / behind / in front of / between / near / next to / over / around / beside / inside

①時を表す前置詞	**in** 2020（2020年に）/ **in** December（12月に）/ **in** summer（夏に）
	on Friday（金曜日に）/ **on** May 1（5月1日に）/ **on** Sunday night（日曜日の夜に）
	at 8 o'clock（8時に）/ **from** ten **to** three（10時から3時まで）/ **since** last year（去年から）/ **until** the end of this week（今週末まで）/ **by** the end of this week（今週末までに）/ **after** five（5時以降）/ **before** dark（暗くなる前に）/ **in** ten minutes（10分で）
	for three months（3カ月間）/ **during** summer vacation（夏休み中）

②場所を表す前置詞	Kai is **in** the office.（カイはオフィスにいます）
	Kai is sitting **on** the sofa and his laptop is **on** his knees. （カイはソファに座り、ノートパソコンは彼の膝の上にあります）
	Kai is sitting **next to** Tom.（カイはトムの隣に座っています）
	Kai's boss is standing **in front of** them.（カイの上司は彼らの前に立っています）
	Linda is walking **to/toward** Kai.（リンダはカイの方へ歩いてきます）
	A clock is **on** the wall **behind** Kai.（カイの後ろの壁に時計が掛けてあります）
	A cabinet is **near** Kai and a vase is **on** the cabinet. （カイの近くにキャビネットがあり、その上に花瓶があります）

Take Note
- at/in/onは「時」と「場所」のどちらも示すことができます。
- on は「〜に接している」という意味を持つので、「机の上に本がある（a book **on** the desk）」「壁にカレンダーがある（a calendar **on** the wall）」「天井にプロジェクターがある（a projector **on** the ceiling）」と言いたい場合にも使われます。
- overや below, down, upは副詞としても使われます。

Grammar **Checkup**

A (   ) 内のa〜cから適当な語句を選んで文を完成させましょう。　⟳CheckLink

1. We're closed for business (a. at b. in c. on) Sundays and holidays.
2. Please don't listen to music (a. during b. on c. to) business hours.
3. The staff meeting starts (a. at b. for c. in) 20 minutes.
4. The small meeting room is (a. near b. next c. beside) to the conference room.
5. There's a copy center (a. on b. in c. to) the 4th floor.
6. The bus stops (a. front b. front of c. in front of) the main entrance.

B 日本語を参考にして、語句を並べ替えて文を完成させましょう。
（文頭の語も小文字になっています）

1. report / next / finish / Friday / by / your （今度の金曜日までに報告書を仕上げてください）

   Please _____.

2. 10 minutes / break / a / take / let's / for （10分間、休憩しましょう）

   _____.

3. you / paper / the / behind / is / copy （コピー用紙はあなたの後ろにあります）

   _____.

4. the / and / it's / elevator / between / Room B12 （それはB12号室とエレベーターの間にあります）

   _____.

C (   ) 内のa〜cから適当な語句を選んで会話を完成させましょう。その後で、音声
を聞いて答えを確認しましょう。　⟳CheckLink 🎧 DL 020 ~ 021 ◉ CD1-20 ~ ◉ CD1-21

1 *At a company orientation* （会社のオリエンテーションで）

A: [1](a. At b. In c. On) nice days, many workers eat [2](a. in b. on c. with)
the park.
B: The park?
A: Yes, there's a small park [3](a. above b. across c. around) the street.

2 *At a company information desk* （会社の受付で）

A: Hello. My name is Dan Jones. I have an appointment with Tom
Brown [1](a. at b. on c. with) 2:00.
B: Yes, Mr. Jones. Mr. Brown's office is [2](a. at b. in c. to) the end of
the hall [3](a. in b. on c. for) your left.

Good Reading

A Googleplexに関する文章を読んで、下のa〜cから適当な語句を選んで空所に書いてみましょう。その後で、音声を聞いて答えを確認しましょう。

Googleplex

Googleplex is the name of the headquarters of Google. It's ¹_____ Mountain View, California, near San Jose. Inside Googleplex, workers have access to gyms, game rooms, laundry rooms, plus many cafeterias and coffee shops. Outside there are organic gardens, swimming pools, tennis courts, sports fields and beach volleyball courts. A popular outdoor attraction ²_____ the main building is Stan, a huge iron tyrannosaurus. ³_____ the day, Google workers often ride colorful bicycles, or "G Bikes," to different Googleplex locations. Many of them also use the free shuttle bus service in the morning and ⁴_____ night.

Notes gyms「体育館、ジム」 iron tyrannosaurus「鉄製のティラノサウルス」

1.	a. to	b. between	c. in
2.	a. in	b. in front of	c. under
3.	a. During	b. On	c. Until
4.	a. in	b. on	c. at

B もう一度文章を読んで質問に最も合う選択肢を選びましょう。   CheckLink

1. What outdoor activity is available at Googleplex?

Ⓐ Golf
Ⓑ Beach volleyball
Ⓒ Fishing
Ⓓ Horseback riding

2. Who is Stan?

Ⓐ A tour guide
Ⓑ A Google gardener
Ⓒ Google's mascot dog
Ⓓ A Googleplex attraction

Writing—About Me

A Kaiの例を参考にして、自分の学校の時間割を書いてみましょう（6限目もあれば空所に書き入れましょう）。

University Timetable	*CompTech University*	
Period 1	9:20 – 10:50	
Period 2	11:05 – 12:35	
Lunch Break	12:35 – 1:20	
Period 3	1:20 – 2:50	
Period 4	3:05 – 4:35	
Period 5	4:50 – 6:20	

B 下の前置詞を使って、Kaiに関する文章を完成させましょう。

after   at   from   in   to

At Kai's university, the first class [1] _____ the morning starts at 9:20. The last class of the day ends [2] _____ 6:20. Classes are 90 minutes long. There's a 15-minute break [3] _____ each class. The lunch break is 45 minutes, [4] _____ 12:35 [5] _____ 1:20. Kai usually eats lunch in the cafeteria.

C **B** を参考にして、自分のことを書いてみましょう。

At my university, the first class _____ .

The last class _____

_____

_____

_____

Fun Times, but...

Grammar	過去時制
Vocabulary	**Entertainment**

Warm-Up Listening

4つの英文を聞いてイラストに最も合っているものを選びましょう。その後で、正解の文を書いてみましょう。 ↻CheckLink 🎧 DL 023 ⊙ CD1-23

Ⓐ　Ⓑ　Ⓒ　Ⓓ　　They're _____.

Word Check

次の英語の意味に合う日本語を選びましょう。　↻CheckLink 🎧 DL 024 ⊙ CD1-24

1. appetizer 　　　(　)
2. colleagues 　　(　)
3. invited 　　　　(　)
4. ordered 　　　　(　)
5. platter 　　　　(　)

a. 前菜
b. 大皿料理、盛り合わせ
c. 招待した
d. 同僚
e. 注文した

Kai's Blog

上の Word Check の語句を使ってKaiのブログを完成させましょう。その後で、音声を聞いて答えを確認しましょう。 🎧 DL 025 ⊙ CD1-25

Yesterday I went out for dinner with two ¹_____. They ²_____ me to a great seafood restaurant. I had a shrimp salad as an ³_____. I ⁴_____ a seafood ⁵_____ for my main dish. For dessert, I had a HUGE chocolate brownie with ice cream. Everything was delicious. ... But I think I ate too much!

Conversation

CheckLink DL 026 CD1-26

A Kaiと同僚2人とのレストランでの会話を聞いて順番に絵を並べましょう。

A

B

C

D

1. [ ] ➡ 2. [ ] ➡ 3. [ ] ➡ 4. [ ]

B もう一度会話を聞いて質問に最も合う選択肢を選びましょう。

CheckLink DL 026 CD1-26

1. What is Kai's problem?

- **A** He doesn't like seafood.
- **B** His stomach hurts.
- **C** He has a headache.
- **D** He doesn't like his dessert.

2. What does Linda tell Kai to do?

- **A** Order another dessert
- **B** Go for a walk
- **C** Take a rest
- **D** Have some water

C もう一度会話を聞いて空所を埋めましょう。   DL 026 CD1-26

Tom: Did you ¹ _____ your meal, Linda?

Linda: Yes, I did. My fish and chips ² _____ delicious.

Tom: My steak was good, too. How about you, Kai? ³ _____ you like your food? … Kai? Are you OK?

Kai: Oh, sorry. Yeah, the food ⁴ _____ fantastic, especially the brownie and ice cream. It ⁵ _____ soooo good! But I think I ⁶ _____ too much. I have a stomachache.

Linda: That's too bad. Here, Kai, drink some water.

Kai: Thanks, Linda.

Waiter: … Last order. Does anyone want more coffee or another dessert? *(to Kai)* Another brownie and ice cream for you, sir?

Kai: No more food, please.

Note especially「特に」

使い方のPOINT

過去時制は主に過去の次のようなことを表す場合に使われます。
- ①終わっている行動や過去の出来事
- ②過去の状況（状態）

①終わっている行動・過去の出来事	Kai **went** to a concert yesterday. （カイは昨日コンサートに行きました） Kai **was** excited at the concert. （カイはコンサートに興奮しました） Kai **bought** two tickets for the musical. （カイはそのミュージカルのチケットを2枚買いました）
②過去の状況（状態）	We **stayed** home and **watched** a movie. （私たちは家にいて、映画を見ました） She **was** a famous movie star. （彼女は有名な映画スターでした）

形　式

be動詞	肯定文	I **was** / You **were** / He/She/It **was**	a musician/great.	
	否定文	I **wasn't** / You **weren't** / He/She/It **wasn't**		
	疑問文	**Was** I / **Were** you / **Was** he/she/it	a musician/great**?**	
	肯定文	We/You/They **were**	musicians/great.	
	否定文	We/You/They **weren't**		
	疑問文	**Were** we/you/they	musicians/great**?**	
一般動詞	肯定文	I/You/We/They **watched**	the movie.	
	否定文	I/You/We/They **didn't watch**		
	疑問文	**Did** I/you/we/they **watch**	the movie**?**	
	肯定文	He/She/It **watched**	the movie.	
	否定文	He/She/It **didn't watch**		
	疑問文	**Did** he/she/it **watch**	the movie**?**	

動詞の-(e)dの付け方（過去形の語尾変化のパターン）

watch→watch**ed**, visit→visit**ed**	語尾にedをつける
please→please**d**, like→like**d**	語尾がeの動詞にはdを付ける
carry→carr**ied**, try→tr**ied**	語尾が子音＋yの動詞はyをiedに変える
beg→be**gg**ed, plan→pla**nn**ed, stop→sto**pp**ed	語尾の子音を2つ重ねる（子音の前の母音が短い音の場合）
make→**made**, go→**went**, come→**came**	不規則な変化をする
put→**put**, cut→**cut**, set→**set**	変化しない

Take Note
- 過去形は過去を示す単語と使うか、過去のこととわかる文脈で使います。

   I went to the movie with her **last Saturday**.（私は先週の土曜日に彼女と映画に行きました）
- 過去の一定の期間を示すことができます。

   The live music club was open **all night last Friday**.
   （ライブハウスは先週の金曜日一晩中開いていました）

Grammar **Checkup**

A ( ) 内のa〜cから適当な語句を選んで文を完成させましょう。 ↻CheckLink

1. Don (**a.** take **b.** taken **c.** took) his son to a soccer game on Sunday.
2. (**a.** Are you went **b.** Did you go **c.** Did you went) to Greg's party?
3. (**a.** Are **b.** Did **c.** Was) the food at the new Italian restaurant good?
4. We (**a.** really enjoyed **b.** were really enjoy **c.** did really enjoyed) the parade.
5. The movie (**a.** didn't end **b.** wasn't end **c.** didn't ended) until midnight.
6. I (**a.** looked **b.** saw **c.** watched) many beautiful pictures at the museum.

B 日本語を参考にして、語句を並べ替えて文を完成させましょう。
（文頭の語も小文字になっています）

1. enjoyable / party / the / very / welcome / was （歓迎会はとても楽しかったです）

_____.

2. a / six / table / Anne / reserved / for （Anneは6人でテーブルを予約しました）

_____.

3. the musical / New York / did / in / enjoy / you
（あなたはニューヨークでミュージカルを楽しみましたか）

_____?

4. it / the picnic / we / rained, / canceled / so （雨が降ったので、私たちはピクニックを中止しました）

_____.

C ( ) 内のa〜cから適当な語句を選んで会話を完成させましょう。その後で、音声
を聞いて答えを確認しましょう。 ↻CheckLink 🎧 DL 027 ~ 028 ◎CD1-27 ~ ◎CD1-28

1 *Two friends talking* （友人どうしの会話）

A: [1](**a.** Did you get **b.** Did you got **c.** Were you get) tickets to the concert?
B: Yes, I [2](**a.** buy **b.** bought **c.** was bought) two tickets online this
morning. But all of the good seats [3](**a.** was **b.** did **c.** were) sold out.
Our seats are far from the stage.

2 *Two colleagues talking* （同僚どうしの会話）

A: How [1](**a.** are **b.** did **c.** was) your weekend, Jake?
B: Good. Alice and I [2](**a.** are going **b.** have gone **c.** went) bowling.
A: I [3](**a.** didn't know **b.** don't know **c.** didn't knew) you liked bowling.
B: I don't. But, Alice loves it.

Good Reading

A サンフランシスコのケーブルカーに関する文章を読んで、下のa～cから適当な語句を選んで空所に書いてみましょう。その後で、音声を聞いて答えを確認しましょう。

The San Francisco Cable Cars

On a wet summer day in 1869, Andrew Smith Hallidie saw a terrible accident. A horse-drawn streetcar with many people inside slid down a hill in San Francisco. All five horses ¹_____. This event ²_____ Hallidie the idea for a cable car system. Between 1873 and 1890, the city built 23 lines. For more than 30 years, the cable car ³_____ the city's main transportation system. There are only three lines now, but the cable cars remain an important part of the city's history. In 2019, seven million people, mostly tourists, ⁴_____ them.

Notes horse-drawn streetcar「鉄道馬車」 slid「滑った（slideの過去形）」 transportation system「交通機関」

1.	**a.** die	**b.** died	**c.** were died
2.	**a.** gave	**b.** received	**c.** took
3.	**a.** had	**b.** did	**c.** was
4.	**a.** ride	**b.** ridden	**c.** rode

B もう一度文章を読んで質問に最も合う選択肢を選びましょう。 CheckLink

1. What gave Mr. Hallidie the idea for a cable car system?

- **A** A streetcar
- **B** A horse race
- **C** Tourists
- **D** An accident

2. How many cable car lines does San Francisco have today?

- **A** One
- **B** Three
- **C** Twenty-three
- **D** Thirty

Writing—About Me

A Kaiの例を参考にして、最近自分のした楽しいことを書いてみましょう。

	Kai	You
Entertainment type	baseball game	
Time of activity	last Sunday	
Location of activity	Oracle Park, San Francisco	
Other information	• San Francisco Giants vs. New York Yankees • great game, Giants won 6-5 • ate hot dogs, drank cola	

B 下の動詞を過去形に変えて、Kaiに関する文章を完成させましょう。

be   go   have   play   win

I ^{1} _____ to a baseball game with my host father and host brother last Sunday. The game ^{2} _____ at Oracle Park in San Francisco. The San Francisco Giants ^{3} _____ the New York Yankees. It was a great game. The Giants ^{4} _____ 6 to 5. During the game, we ^{5} _____ hot dogs and cola.

C **B** を参考にして、最近自分のした楽しいことを書いてみましょう。

I _____

_____

_____

_____

_____

Hints　スポーツイベント、コンサート、美術館、ショッピング、楽しい場所

They Look Good on You

Grammar	可算・不可算名詞
Vocabulary	**Shopping**

Warm-Up Listening

4つの英文を聞いてイラストに最も合っているものを選びましょう。その後で、正解の文を書いてみましょう。　CheckLink　DL 030　CD1-30

Ⓐ　Ⓑ　Ⓒ　Ⓓ　　Kai _____.

Word Check

次の英語の意味に合う日本語を選びましょう。　CheckLink　DL 031　CD1-31

1. on sale 　　(　)
2. payment 　　(　)
3. quality 　　(　)
4. reasonable 　　(　)
5. selection 　　(　)

a. 選ばれたもの、品ぞろえ
b. 品質
c. 支払い
d. 手頃な
e. 発売中、セール中

Kai's Blog

上の　Word Check　の語句を使ってKaiのブログを完成させましょう。
その後で、音声を聞いて答えを確認しましょう。　DL 032　CD1-32

Today I shopped at a menswear store for some casual business clothes.
The store had a large ¹_____ of good ²_____ clothes.
The prices were ³_____, and many items were ⁴_____. The
shopping trip was very successful. The only problem was the ⁵_____. …

A 買い物中のKaiとWendyの会話を聞いて順番に絵を並べましょう。

A

B

C

D

1. ⬜ ➡ 2. ⬜ ➡ 3. ⬜ ➡ 4.

B もう一度会話を聞いて質問に最も合う選択肢を選びましょう。

CheckLink DL 033 CD1-33

1. What shirt colors does Kai choose?

Ⓐ White and gray
Ⓑ Gray and blue
Ⓒ White and blue
Ⓓ Blue and red

2. How much are the clothes?

Ⓐ $90.15
Ⓑ $90.50
Ⓒ $98.15
Ⓓ $98.50

C もう一度会話を聞いて空所を埋めましょう。 DL 033 CD1-33

Wendy: Those ¹ _____ look good on you Kai.

Kai: Yeah, I like them, too. And they're very comfortable.

Wendy: *(a few minutes later)* Do you need anything else?

Kai: Well, I need a couple of ² _____ for work.

Wendy: The ³ _____ on this rack are all 50% off.

Kai: Oh, good. … Do you like this ⁴ _____?

Wendy: Yes, it's very nice. And it's the right size.

Kai: OK. I like the navy one and the white one. *(goes to cashier)*

Cashier: That's ninety-eight dollars and fifty cents, please.

Kai: … Oh, no. Wendy, I don't have enough ⁵ _____.

Wendy: How ⁶ _____ do you need?

Kai: Ninety-eight dollars and fifty cents. … I forgot my wallet.

使い方のPOINT

名詞には数えられる名詞と数えられない名詞があります。

数えられる名詞

①単数の名詞にはa/anがつく
②複数の名詞には-sがつくものと、語尾が変化して-(e)sがつくものがある
③some/any/manyがつくことができる
④異なる複数形を持つ名詞がある

数えられない名詞

⑤数えられない名詞には集合名詞（まとまり）、抽象名詞（抽象的なもの）がある
⑥some/any/muchがつくことができる
⑦数える場合に使う表現がある
⑧通常、複数形で使う名詞がある（複数形で1つのものを示す）

数えられる名詞	
①単数形 （a/an＋名詞）	**a** shirt / **a** handbag
	a glass / **a** dish / **a** strawberry / **a** knife / **a** shelf
	an item / **an** umbrella / **an** hour
②複数形	shirt**s** / handbag**s** / item**s** / umbrella**s** / hour**s**
	glass**es** / dish**es** / strawberr**ies** / kni**ves** / shel**ves**
③some/any/many	**some** shirts / **some** glasses / **some** items
	any shirts / **any** glasses / **any** items
	many shirts / **many** glasses / **many** items
④異なる複数形	man-**men** / woman-**women** / child-**children** / foot-**feet**

数えられない名詞	
⑤まとまり	water / coffee / tea / juice / oil
	meat / furniture / staff
	bread / sugar / luggage
抽象的なもの	money / information / fun
⑥some/any/much	**some** water / **some** furniture / **some** bread / **some** money
	any water / **any** furniture / **any** bread / **any** information
	much water / **much** furniture / **much** money / **much** sugar
⑦数える表現	**a glass of** water（コップ1杯の水）/ **a bottle of** wine（1本のワイン）/ **a cup of** coffee/tea（1杯のコーヒー/お茶）/ **a spoonful of** sugar（ひとさじの砂糖）/ **a piece of** information（ひとつの情報）/ **a slice of** bread（ひと切れのパン）/ **a pair of** shoes（1足の靴）
⑧複数形で使う名詞	shoes / scissors / pants / glasses / jeans / pyjamas

Take Note

● 数えられる名詞を代名詞で示すときには one か ones を使うことができます。

Shall I buy the red **cups** or the green **ones**?
（赤いカップを買いましょうか、緑のものにしましょうか）

I'm going to buy **a drink**. Do you want **one**?
（私は飲み物を買ってきます。あなたも欲しいですか）

Grammar Checkup

A (　　) 内のa～cから適当な語句を選んで文を完成させましょう。　CheckLink

1. Let's buy (a. a food b. foods c. some food) for the party.
2. Does this store sell (a. furniture b. furnitures c. a furniture)?
3. (a. This pants is b. These pants are c. This pants are) 25% off today.
4. She bought (a. a bread b. some bread c. a breads) at the bakery.
5. I need a new (a. shoes b. pair of shoe c. pair of shoes).
6. Jim always pays in (a. cash b. money c. dollar).

B 日本語を参考にして、語句を並べ替えて文を完成させましょう。
（文頭の語も小文字になっています）

1. two / milk / bought / liters / I / of （私は2リットルの牛乳を買いました）

   _____.

2. a / come / does / in / medium / this （これのMサイズはありますか）

   _____?

3. you / looks / color / on / good / that （あの色はあなたに似合っています）

   _____.

4. clothes / all / Karen / online / buys / her （Karenは洋服をすべてネットで買います）

   _____.

C (　　) 内のa～cから適当な語句を選んで会話を完成させましょう。その後で、音声を聞いて答えを確認しましょう。　CheckLink　DL 034～035　CD1-34 ～ CD1-35

1 *At a shoe store* （靴店で）

> **A:** Are [1](a. this boot b. these boots c. this boots) on sale?
> **B:** No, they aren't. But the black [2](a. its b. one c. ones) are on sale for $80.
> **A:** Oh, that's [3](a. good price b. a good price c. price is good).

2 *Back from the supermarket* （スーパーマーケットから帰宅して）

> **A:** [1](a. Meat was b. Meat were c. Meats was) on sale today.
> **B:** Did you buy [2](a. one b. ones c. some)?
> **A:** Yes, I bought [3](a. a pork b. some pork c. some porks) and two steaks.

A ジーンズに関する文章を読んで、下のa〜cから適当な語句を選んで空所に書いてみましょう。その後で、音声を聞いて答えを確認しましょう。

BLUE JEANS

Blue jeans have a long ¹_____ in the United States. The "birthday" of blue jeans is May 20, 1873. On that day, Levi Strauss and his business ²_____ Jacob Davis received a patent for the use of copper rivets on the pocket corners of denim pants. The rivets made the pants very strong and durable—perfect for workmen. The two men soon opened a factory in San Francisco. Today, ³_____ almost everywhere in the world wear jeans, from young children to adults. The average American owns not one, but seven ⁴_____! How many do you own?

Notes patent「特許」 copper rivet「銅製リベット」 durable「耐久性のある、丈夫な」

1. a. history	b. time	c. years
2. a. company	b. men	c. partner
3. a. a person	b. someone	c. people
4. a. jeans	b. pairs	c. jean pairs

B もう一度文章を読んで質問に最も合う選択肢を選びましょう。 CheckLink

1. What happened on May 20, 1873?

Ⓐ Levi Strauss was born.
Ⓑ Jacob Davis made the first rivet.
Ⓒ Strauss and Davis became partners.
Ⓓ Strauss and Davis received a patent.

2. What was the purpose of the rivets?

Ⓐ To give the pants more strength
Ⓑ To make the pockets unique
Ⓒ To keep the shape of the pockets
Ⓓ To make the pants fashionable

Writing—About Me

A Wendyの例を参考にして、自分の情報を書いてみましょう。

	Wendy	You
What did you buy last week? How much did they cost?	• bottled water X 2 ($3) • sandals ($20) • sunhat ($15)	
Do you sometimes shop online? If yes, for what?	(Yes) books, concert tickets No	
Do you sometimes buy second-hand things?	(Yes) vintage jeans, T-shirts, etc. No	
What do you want to buy this year?	• tablet computer • game software	

B 下の語句を使って、Wendyに関する文章を完成させましょう。

a bottles clothes pair some

Last week, Wendy bought two ¹_____ of water for $3, a ²_____ of sandals for $20 and ³_____ sunhat for $15. She sometimes shops for books and concert tickets online. She also sometimes buys second-hand vintage ⁴_____. She wants to buy a tablet computer and ⁵_____ game software this year.

C **B** を参考にして、自分のことを書いてみましょう。

Last week, I bought _____

_____

_____

_____

_____

Tech Talk

Grammar	Wh疑問文
Vocabulary	**Technology**

Warm-Up Listening

4つの英文を聞いてイラストに最も合っているものを選びましょう。その後で、正解の文を書いてみましょう。　↻CheckLink　🎧 DL 037　◎ CD1-37

Ⓐ　Ⓑ　Ⓒ　Ⓓ　　Kai _____.

Word Check

次の英語の意味に合う日本語を選びましょう。　↻CheckLink　🎧 DL 038　◎ CD1-38

1. demonstrated　　（　　）　　**a.** 実演した、示した
2. developed　　　（　　）　　**b.** 機器、装置
3. devices　　　　（　　）　　**c.** 開発した
4. features　　　　（　　）　　**d.** 操作した
5. navigated　　　（　　）　　**e.** 特徴、機能

Kai's Blog

上の Word Check の語句を使ってKaiのブログを完成させましょう。その後で、音声を聞いて答えを確認しましょう。　🎧 DL 039　◎ CD1-39

Linda and her team recently [1] _____ a new app. Today Linda [2] _____ it for me. She explained the whole process of creating the app. The app works on both iPhone and Android [3] _____. It has many useful [4] _____. I [5] _____ it easily, and it worked very well. However, I had one very scary moment. …

Conversation

A 新しいアプリについてのKaiとLindaの会話を聞いて順番に絵を並べましょう。

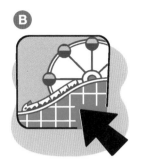

1. ▢ ➡ 2. ▢ ➡ 3. ▢ ➡ 4. ▢

B もう一度会話を聞いて質問に最も合う選択肢を選びましょう。

1. What is Linda's job?

Ⓐ Technology manager
Ⓑ Visual designer
Ⓒ Computer programmer
Ⓓ Systems engineer

2. What did Kai do by clicking on the black cat icon?

Ⓐ Open the app
Ⓑ Delete the program
Ⓒ Start the virtual tour
Ⓓ Save the changes

C もう一度会話を聞いて空所を埋めましょう。　DL 040　CD1-40

Linda: Take a look at some of these visual designs, Kai. I made them for this app.

Kai: OK. ¹＿＿＿＿＿ the ²＿＿＿＿＿ of the app?

Linda: It's *Ride On*.

Kai: Oh. ³＿＿＿＿＿ it ⁴＿＿＿＿＿? A bus company? A taxi company?

Linda: No, it's for an amusement park. Here's the icon for the app.

Kai: It's nice. ⁵＿＿＿＿＿ does it ⁶＿＿＿＿＿?

Linda: Well, there's a park map with a virtual tour. It tells you the waiting time for each attraction. It also has links to all of the restaurants and tells you how crowded they are.

Kai: Sounds cool! What does this black cat icon do? *(He taps it.)*

Linda: Oh, no, you just deleted the program. And I didn't save it!

Kai: Oh my gosh! Really?

Linda: Just kidding. You just saved the changes. Sorry for scaring you.

Notes delete「削除する」　just kidding「ただの冗談」　scare「怖がらせる」

使い方のPOINT

when / where / who / how / which / why / whatを用いたWh疑問文では、以下のことを尋ねることができます。

①時（when）　②場所（where）　③誰（who）　④手段・方法／程度（how）
⑤どちらか（which）　⑥理由（why）　⑦何か（what）

①時	**When** did you print out the report? （いつあなたはレポートをプリントアウトしましたか） **When** do they have their online meetings? （いつ彼らはオンライン会議をしますか）
②場所	**Where** did you get your new PC? （どこであなたは新しいパソコンを買いましたか） **Where** is the IT manager? （どこにIT部長はいますか）
③誰	**Who** is responsible for computer hardware? （誰がコンピューターのハードウェアの責任がありますか） **Who** upgraded your Internet service? （誰がインターネットサービスをアップグレードしましたか）
④手段・方法／程度	**How** does this 3-D printer work? （どのようにしてこの3Dプリンタは機能しますか） **How** long did it take to install the software? （そのソフトウェアをインストールするのにどれくらいかかりましたか） **How** often do you check your mobile phone a day? （あなたは1日にどれくらい携帯電話をチェックしますか）
⑤どちらか	**Which** software did you choose? （どのソフトウエアをあなたは選びましたか） **Which** icon does Kai like?　（どのアイコンがカイは好きですか）
⑥理由	**Why** did you switch from Windows to Mac? （なぜあなたはWindowsからMacに替えたのですか） **Why** did they develop this software? （なぜ彼らはこのソフトウェアを開発したのですか）
⑦何か	**What** do you buy in the e-store? （何をあなたはEストアで買いますか） **What** is your favorite app? （あなたの好きなアプリは何ですか） **What** time does the teleconference begin? （何時に電話会議は始まりますか）

 Take Note　● 「どの〜」を尋ねたい場合、あらかじめ選ぶものがあるときはwhich、ないときはwhatを使います。
　Which app do you usually use, Twitter or Instagram?
　（ツイッターとインスタグラム、どのアプリをいつも使いますか）
　What app do you usually use?　（どのアプリをいつも使いますか）

Grammar **Checkup**

A (   ) 内のa～cから適当な語句を選んで文を完成させましょう。　　　⟲CheckLink

1. (a. How b. What c. Who) do you make a music playlist?

2. (a. What kind b. Where c. Which) podcasts do you listen to?

3. (a. How b. What c. Why) is my browser so slow?

4. (a. What b. Where c. Which) is Wi-Fi available on campus?

5. (a. How b. What c. When) time does the live streaming of the concert start?

6. Who (a. hacked b. is hacker c. is hacking person) into the computer system?

B 日本語を参考にして、語句を並べ替えて文を完成させましょう。
（文頭の語も小文字になっています）

1. the / software / installed / who / new / computer
（誰がその新しいコンピューターソフトをインストールしましたか）

_____?

2. send / when / the file / you / did / me （いつあなたは私にそのファイルを送りましたか）

_____?

3. of / it / what / tablet / is / kind （それはどんな種類のタブレットですか）

_____?

4. back up / how / your files / do / often / you
（どのくらいの頻度であなたはファイルのバックアップを取りますか）

_____?

C (   ) 内のa～cから適当な語句を選んで会話を完成させましょう。その後で、音声
を聞いて答えを確認しましょう。　⟲CheckLink　🎧 DL 041 ~ 042　◉ CD1-41 ~ ◉ CD1-42

1 *At an electronics store* （電器店で）

A: [1](a. How b. Where c. Which) do you prefer, desktops or laptops?
B: Laptops.
A: [2](a. What b. Which c. Why) do you like laptops?
B: They're portable. [3](a. How b. What c. Where) do you think of this one?

2 *In a car* （車内で）

A: [1](a. What b. Where c. Who) are we? Let's check the GPS.
B: OK. ...[2](a. What's b. Where's c. Who's) the name of the restaurant?
A: It's Gusta Pizza.
B: [3](a. How b. What c. Which) do you spell that? G-O-O-S-T-A?
A: No, it's G-U-S-T-A, I think. ... Here it is. It's on the other side of town!

Good Reading

A アプリに関する文章を読んで、下のa〜cから適当な語句を選んで空所に書いてみましょう。その後で、音声を聞いて答えを確認しましょう。

App Basics

1. _____ is a mobile app?

It's a software program. You download and access it on your phone or other mobile device.

2. _____ did the first app appear?

In 1997. Nokia Corporation of Finland included a built-in version of the basic arcade game "Snake" on its Nokia 6110 mobile phone.

3. _____ are some apps free?

Some app developers earn money from advertising within the app. Other developers provide a basic free app and hope users buy an upgrade later.

4. _____ time do people spend in apps?

About ninety percent of smartphone use is in apps, especially digital audio, digital video and social media.

Note arcade game「ゲームセンターのゲーム (機)」

1.	a. What	b. Where	c. Who
2.	a. Why	b. When	c. Where
3.	a. What kind	b. Which	c. Why
4.	a. What	b. How much	c. How

B もう一度文章を読んで質問に最も合う選択肢を選びましょう。　CheckLink

1. What is "Snake"?

Ⓐ A game
Ⓑ A mobile phone series
Ⓒ A company in Finland
Ⓓ A character in an arcade game

2. For every 100 minutes of smartphone use, how much is spent in apps?

Ⓐ About 10 minutes
Ⓑ About 20 minutes
Ⓒ About 50 minutes
Ⓓ About 90 minutes

Writing—About Me

A Kaiの例を参考にして、自分の情報を書いてみましょう
（スマートフォン以外で考えてみましょう）。

	Kai	You
What's an electrical product that you use?	refrigerator	
When did you or your family get it?	5 years ago	
How often do you use it?	about 10 times/day	
Why do you like it?	• keeps food fresh & cool • freezer section allows storage for a long time • not necessary to shop for food every day	

B 下の語句を使って、Kaiに関する文章を完成させましょう。

family   ice cream   item   reasons   times

A refrigerator is an important electrical [1] _____ for me. My
[2] _____ got a new one five years ago. I use it about ten
[3] _____ a day. I like it for three [4] _____ :

1) It keeps food fresh and cool.
2) The freezer section can store food such as meat and [5] _____ for a long time.
3) With a refrigerator, it isn't necessary to shop for food every day.

C **B** を参考にして、自分のことを書いてみましょう。

_____ is an important _____
_____

I like it for three reasons:
1) _____
2) _____
3) _____

You're Sitting on It...

Grammar	進行形
Vocabulary	**Daily life**

Warm-Up Listening

4つの英文を聞いてイラストに最も合っているものを選びましょう。その後で、正解の文を書いてみましょう。　🔄CheckLink　🎧DL 044　💿CD1-44

Ⓐ Ⓑ Ⓒ Ⓓ _____ is _____.

Word Check

次の英語の意味に合う日本語を選びましょう。　🔄CheckLink　🎧DL 045　💿CD1-45

1. ceiling （　　）
2. covering （　　）
3. laying （　　）
4. preparing （　　）
5. wiping （　　）

a. 置いている、敷いている
b. 天井
c. ふいている
d. 準備している
e. 覆っている、かぶせている

Kai's Blog

上の Word Check の語句を使ってKaiのブログを完成させましょう。その後で、音声を聞いて答えを確認しましょう。　🎧DL 046　💿CD1-46

This morning, Wendy was ¹_____ to paint her bedroom. Everyone was helping her. Mr. Nelson and Brian were moving large pieces of furniture into the center of the room, and ²_____ them with a plastic sheet. Mrs. Nelson was ³_____ newspaper on the floor. Wendy was putting small things into boxes. And I was ⁴_____ the walls and ⁵_____. Everything went smoothly … this morning.

A 部屋の模様替えについてのKaiとWendyとの会話を聞いて順番に絵を並べましょう。

A  B  C  D

1. ⇒ 2. ⇒ 3. ⇒ 4.

B もう一度会話を聞いて質問に最も合う選択肢を選びましょう。

CheckLink   DL 047   CD1-47

1. What was Wendy looking for?

- **A** A paint brush
- **B** A paint roller
- **C** A list
- **D** A face mask

2. Who knows how to use a paint roller?

- **A** Only Kai
- **B** Only Wendy
- **C** Both Kai and Wendy
- **D** Wendy's father

C もう一度会話を聞いて空所を埋めましょう。   DL 047   CD1-47

Kai: What are you doing Wendy?

Wendy: I'm ¹ _____ for my pre-painting checklist. You're ² _____ on it …

Kai: Oh, sorry. … Here you are.

Wendy: Thanks. Number 1: Are you ³ _____ old clothes and a face mask?

Kai: Oops. I'm ⁴ _____ wearing my face mask.

Wendy: OK, put it on. Number 2: Are your windows open?

Kai: I'm ⁵ _____ them now.

Wendy: Thanks. Number 3: Are you ⁶ _____ a paint brush or a paint roller?

Kai: A paint roller?

Wendy: That's right. Do you know how to use a paint roller, Kai?

Kai: No. Do you?

Wendy: No, but I know someone who does. … Daaaad!

使い方のPOINT

進行形は次のようなことを表す場合に使われます。

現在進行形

①いま起こっていること　②一時的に起きていること　③近い未来のこと

過去進行形

④過去に起きている動作　⑤過去に起こっている状況

①いま起こっていること	I **am washing** dishes.（私はお皿を洗っています） She **is eating** breakfast now.（彼女はいま朝食を食べています）
②一時的に起きていること	This week, Kai **is taking** a bus to school. （今週、カイはバスで通学しています）
③近い未来のこと	Kai **is painting** his room this weekend. （今週末、カイは部屋のペンキを塗ります） He **is going** to the doctor tomorrow. （明日、彼は医者に行く予定です）
④過去に起きている動作	Wendy **was watching** TV with her brother yesterday. （昨日、ウェンディは弟とテレビを見ていました） Mr. Nelson **was driving** home from work. （ネルソンさんは仕事場から家に車で帰っているところでした）
⑤過去に起こっている状況	My father **was repairing** his computer here yesterday. （昨日、父はここでコンピュータの修理をしていました） They **were digging** up the road in front of our house for two days. （彼らは私たちの家の前の道路を2日間掘り返していました）

形　式				
現在進行形	肯定文	I	**am washing**	dishes.
		You/We/They	**are washing**	
		He/She	**is washing**	
	否定文	I	**'m not washing**	
		You/We/They	**aren't washing**	
		He/She	**isn't washing**	
	疑問文	**Am** I		dishes**?**
		Are you/we/they	**washing**	
		Is he/she		
過去進行形	肯定文	I	**was washing**	dishes.
		You/We/They	**were washing**	
		He/She	**was washing**	
	否定文	I	**wasn't washing**	
		You/We/They	**weren't washing**	
		He/She	**wasn't washing**	
	疑問文	**Was** I		dishes**?**
		Were you/we/they	**washing**	
		Was he/she		

Take Note ● 進行形と一緒に使われる語句には now や at the moment（目下）のほか、this week や this year など特定の時期を示すものなどがあります。

Grammar **Checkup**

CheckLink

A (   ) 内の a 〜 c から適当な語句を選んで文を完成させましょう。

1. The workers (a. are b. is c. do) repairing the road now.
2. My toaster (a. doesn't working b. isn't work c. isn't working).
3. Why (a. is the train stopping b. is stopping the train c. the train is stopping)?
4. (a. Are b. Do c. Were) Ed and Ann washing the windows yesterday?
5. (a. What's reading Helen b. What's Helen reading c. What are Helen reading)?
6. No one (a. are b. is c. isn't) checking the heating system these days.

B 日本語を参考にして、語句を並べ替えて文を完成させましょう。
（文頭の語も小文字になっています）

1. replacing / am / I / flooring / old / my （私は私の古いフローリングを取り替えています）

   _____.

2. gas / checking / workers / lines / are / city （市役所の職員がガス管を点検しています）

   _____.

3. your / then / was / connection / working / Internet
   （そのとき、あなたのインターネット接続は機能していましたか）

   _____?

4. on / were / volunteers / picking up / the beach / trash
   （ボランティアがビーチでゴミ拾いをしていました）

   _____.

C (   ) 内の a 〜 c から適当な語句を選んで会話を完成させましょう。その後で、音声
を聞いて答えを確認しましょう。 CheckLink DL 048 〜 049 CD1-48 〜 CD1-49

1 *At the office* （オフィスで）

A: What [1](a. are doing you b. are you doing c. you're doing), Cathy?
B: [2](a. The fan is cleaning b. It's cleaning the fan c. I'm cleaning the fan).
   [3](a. It was b. It were c. It's was) making a strange noise.

2 *At home* （家で）

A: [1](a. Did b. Had c. Were) you looking for something in the garage, Mike?
B: No, I [2](a. was fixing b. did fixing c. was fixed) my bicycle tire.
   [3](a. I'm coming home b. I home was coming c. I was coming home)
   last night, and I rode over some glass.

Good Reading

A DIYに関する文章を読んで、下のa〜cから適当な語句を選んで空所に書いてみましょう。その後で、音声を聞いて答えを確認しましょう。

DIY

These days, "do-it-yourself" (DIY) is becoming more and more popular in Japan. In the early 1970s, there were only a few home centers in the country.　Now there are about five thousand.　Today, many people are ¹_____ and wallpapering rooms, repairing cracks in walls and water pipes, building patios and wood decks, or ²_____ broken toasters and watches. Other people are making their own clothing, transforming old kimonos, shirts and jeans into unique bags, or ³_____ original jewelry and accessories.　With DIY, people are not only ⁴_____ money, they are also learning new things and gaining personal satisfaction.

Notes crack「ひび、割れ目」 patio「中庭」 jewelry「宝石類」 not only ...「…だけでなく」 gain「手に入れる」

1. a. drawing	**b.** painting	**c.** writing
2. a. fixing	**b.** making	**c.** buying
3. a. creating	**b.** finding	**c.** starting
4. a. spending	**b.** collecting	**c.** saving

B もう一度文章を読んで質問に最も合う選択肢を選びましょう。　CheckLink

1. How many home centers are there in Japan?

- **Ⓐ** About 50
- **Ⓑ** About 500
- **Ⓒ** About 1,500
- **Ⓓ** About 5,000

2. In line 10, what does the word "transforming" mean?

- **Ⓐ** Wearing
- **Ⓑ** Cutting
- **Ⓒ** Changing
- **Ⓓ** Putting

Writing—About Me

A Kaiの例を参考にして、自分の情報を書いてみましょう。

Body Maintenance Check	Kai	You
How many hours are you sleeping every night?	about 8 hours	
What are you having for breakfast these days?	toast or cereal	
How much water are you drinking every day?	about 1 liter	
What kind of exercise are you doing? How often?	weightlifting—3 times a week for 30 minutes	
Are you using sunscreen every day?	no	
Are you cleaning your teeth after every meal?	yes	

B 下の進行形を使って、Kaiに関する文章を完成させましょう。

brushing   eating   getting   lifting   protecting

These days, Kai is ¹ _____ about 8 hours of sleep a night. He's ² _____ toast or cereal for breakfast, and drinking about 1 liter of water every day. He's ³ _____ weights 3 times a week for 30 minutes. He isn't ⁴ _____ his skin with sunscreen. He's ⁵ _____ his teeth after every meal.

C **B** を参考にして、自分のことを書いてみましょう。

These days, I'm _____

_____

_____

_____

_____

Unit 8

Going Green

Grammar	助動詞
Vocabulary	**Environment**

Warm-Up Listening

4つの英文を聞いてイラストに最も合っているものを選びましょう。その後で、正解の文を書いてみましょう。　⟳CheckLink　🎧 DL 051　◎ CD1-51

Ⓐ　Ⓑ　Ⓒ　Ⓓ　　There are _____.

Word Check

次の英語の意味に合う日本語を選びましょう。　⟳CheckLink　🎧 DL 052　◎ CD1-52

1. litter　　　　　　　　（　　）
2. natural beauty　　　（　　）
3. rolling　　　　　　　（　　）
4. sandy　　　　　　　（　　）
5. waterfalls　　　　　（　　）

a. 滝
b. なだらかな起伏のある
c. 砂の
d. 自然美
e. （ポイ捨てされた）ゴミ

Kai's Blog

上の Word Check の語句を使ってKaiのブログを完成させましょう。その後で、音声を聞いて答えを確認しましょう。　🎧 DL 053　◎ CD1-53

The San Francisco Bay Area is full of [1]_____. You can enjoy everything from [2]_____ and [3]_____ beaches to mountains and [4]_____ hills. Today I visited one of the beaches—not to swim or lie on the sand, but to clean up some of the [5]_____. The first thing I had to clean up, however, was myself. …

Conversation

A KaiとLindaのビーチの清掃についての会話を聞いて順番に絵を並べましょう。

A

B

Cans
Plastic bottles
Plastic bags
Paper bags
Plastic cups

C

Keep
Our
Beaches
Clean

D

Water

1. ⬜ ➡ 2. ⬜ ➡ 3. ⬜ ➡ 4. ⬜

B もう一度会話を聞いて質問に最も合う選択肢を選びましょう。

1. How often does Linda's company do beach cleanups?

- **A** Once a week
- **B** Once a month
- **C** Twice a year
- **D** Four times a year

2. What is the last thing Kai puts on?

- **A** Sunscreen
- **B** Sunglasses
- **C** A cap
- **D** A face mask

C もう一度会話を聞いて空所を埋めましょう。 DL 054 CD1-54

Linda: I'm glad you ¹_____ join us today for the company's monthly beach cleanup.

Kai: You ²_____ have to thank me. I'm happy to volunteer.

Linda: Great. Here are the supplies you need—a trash bag, tongs and gloves.

Kai: ³_____ I just put everything in the bag?

Linda: That's right. And you also have to ⁴_____ this data sheet. It lists everything you might ⁵_____.

Kai: All right. Is that all?

Linda: Yes. Here's some water. And you ⁶_____ put on this sunscreen.

Kai: Good idea. ... OK, finished.

Linda: Then let's get started. ... Be careful Kai. It's ...

Kai: Whoa!

Linda: ... slippery.

Note tongs「トング」

Grammar **Menu**

使い方の**POINT**

助動詞は動詞の補助をして次のような意味を加えます。後ろには動詞の原形が続きます。
　①可能性・能力（〜できる）　②義務（〜ねばならない）
　③許可（〜してもよい）　④話し手の気持ち（〜したほうがよい、〜すべき）
　⑤推量（〜だろう、〜かもしれない）　⑥必然（〜にちがいない、〜のはずがない）

①可能性・能力 （〜できる）	You **can** buy organic food at the store. （あなたはそのお店で自然食品を買うことができます） We **can't** ignore global warming anymore. （私たちはこれ以上地球温暖化を無視することはできません） They **couldn't** find any trash cans on the beach. （彼らはビーチに空きカンを見つけることができませんでした）
②義務 （〜ねばならない）	We **must/have to** use green products. （私たちは環境にやさしい製品を使わなければなりません） You **don't have to** buy new clothes so often. （あなたはそんなに頻ぱんに新しい洋服を買う必要はありません） The man threw garbage into the river and **had to** pay a $50 fine. （その男性は川にゴミを捨てて50ドルの罰金を払わなければなりませんでした）
③許可 （〜してもよい）	You **may** use these bicycles for free. （あなたはこの自転車を無料で使っても構いません） You **may not** fish in this lake. （この湖で魚を捕ってはいけません） **May** I turn up the heat?（温度を上げてもよいですか） **Can** I use my eco-bag? （自分のエコバッグを使ってよいですか）
④話し手の気持ち （〜したほうがよい、 〜すべき）	You **had better/ought to** use green products. （あなたは環境にやさしい製品を使うべきです） You **had better not** use this product. （あなたはこの製品を使うべきではありません） You **should** use green products. （あなたは環境にやさしい製品を使ったほうがよいでしょう） You **shouldn't** use this product. （あなたはこの製品を使わないほうがよいでしょう） You **must not** use this product. （あなたはこの製品を使ってはいけません）
⑤推量 （〜だろう、〜かも しれない）	The new system **may** save a lot of water and energy. （その新しいシステムは多くの水とエネルギーを節約するかもしれません） People **might** use public bicycles more and more in the future. （人びとは将来、ますますシェアサイクルを利用するかもしれません）
⑥必然 （〜にちがいない、 〜のはずがない）	This product **must** be environmentally friendly. （この製品は環境にやさしいにちがいありません） Air pollution **can't** be good for us. （大気汚染が私たちにとってよいはずはありません）

 ● 「〜してもよいですか」と尋ねたい場合、Can I 〜 ?はカジュアル、May I 〜 ?はていねいな表現になります。また、may notは会話ではあまり使われず、can'tがよく使われます。

Grammar **Checkup**

A ( ) 内のa～cから適当な語句を選んで文を完成させましょう。　⟲CheckLink

1. The company can (**a.** recycle **b.** recycles **c.** recycling) most paper products.

2. We (**a.** must **b.** ought **c.** should) to do more to protect the environment.

3. I (**a.** can't **b.** might not **c.** couldn't) find any organic vegetables yesterday.

4. Electric cars (**a.** has to **b.** may **c.** should to) become very popular one day.

5. You (**a.** don't have to **b.** must **c.** shouldn't) use an eco-bag, but it's a good idea.

6. People (**a.** can't **b.** shouldn't **c.** should) never throw garbage in the street.

B 日本語を参考にして、語句を並べ替えて文を完成させましょう。
（文頭の語も小文字になっています）

1. the / have / trash / we / separate / to　（私たちはゴミを分けなければなりません）

   _____.

2. pollution / may / air / this / reduce / law　（この法律は大気汚染を減らすかもしれません）

   _____.

3. to / low-energy / you / use / light bulbs / ought　（低エネルギーの電球を使うべきです）

   _____.

4. the / problem / planting trees / help with / global warming / can
   （木を植えることは地球温暖化の問題に役立つ可能性があります）

   _____.

C ( ) 内のa～cから適当な語句を選んで会話を完成させましょう。その後で、音声
を聞いて答えを確認しましょう。　⟲CheckLink　🎧 DL 055～056　◎CD1-55 ～ ◎CD1-56

1 *In a coffee shop* （コーヒーショップで）

> **A:** This café [1](**a.** might **b.** have to **c.** ought) stop using plastic straws.
> **B:** I think it [2](**a.** have to **b.** don't have to **c.** should). And it [3](**a.** couldn't
> **b.** shouldn't **c.** can) use plastic cups, either.

2 *At a lake* （湖で）

> **A:** [1](**a.** May **b.** Can **c.** Should) you read the sign, Kai? It says "NO
> SWIMMING."
> **B:** The water [2](**a.** must not **b.** shouldn't **c.** doesn't have to) be safe. We
> [3](**a.** couldn't **b.** has to **c.** ought to) find another place. Let's look at
> the map.

Good Reading

A ビーチの清掃に関する文章を読んで、下のa〜cから適当な語句を選んで空所に書いてみましょう。その後で、音声を聞いて答えを確認しましょう。

Before & After

Afroz Shah was a young lawyer from Mumbai, India. In 2015, he bought a new apartment overlooking the sea. But he ¹_____ see any sand. Trash covered the entire 2.5 km-long beach. Mr. Shah knew that he ²_____ take action. Every weekend, he and his 84-year-old neighbor picked up trash along the beach. One day, two men said to Mr. Shah, "Please, sir, ³_____ we wear your gloves?" Over time, more than 1,000 volunteers joined Mr. Shah and removed millions of kilograms of trash. Twenty-one months later, they ⁴_____ look for trash anymore. All you could see … was sand.

Notes overlooking「見下ろしている」
neighbor「隣人」

Photo courtesy of MYGREENMUM.COM
(https://mygreenmum.com/unique-earth-friendly-products/)

1.	a. can	b. could	c. couldn't
2.	a. had to	b. has to	c. have to
3.	a. can	b. should	c. must
4.	a. didn't have to	b. must	c. should

B もう一度文章を読んで質問に最も合う選択肢を選びましょう。　CheckLink

1. How often did Mr. Shah and his neighbor collect trash?

Ⓐ Every day
Ⓑ Every weekend
Ⓒ Once a month
Ⓓ Twice a month

2. How long did the cleanup project take?

Ⓐ About twenty-one weeks
Ⓑ About one year
Ⓒ Almost two years
Ⓓ More than four years

Writing—About Me

A 環境を守るための行動に関する Kai の意見を参考にして、自分の考えを書いて
みましょう（下の写真も参考にしましょう）。

Kai thinks we should (○) / shouldn't (×)...		I think we should (○) / shouldn't (×)...	
○	buy organic vegetables	○	
○	read more e-books/e-magazines	○	
×	take long showers	×	
×	throw away food	×	

electric cars   plastic bags   unnecessary things

forests   lights   wild animals

B 下の語句を使って、Kai に関する文章を完成させましょう。

a good idea   never   not good   ought   should

To help protect the environment, Kai thinks we
¹ _____ to buy organic vegetables. He also believes
that it's ² _____ to read more e-books and
e-magazines. He thinks that it's ³ _____ to take
long showers, and that we ⁴ _____ ⁵ _____ throw away food.

C **B** を参考にして、自分のことを書いてみましょう。

To help protect the environment, I think _____
_____
_____
_____
_____

Time to Work

Grammar	Will & Be going to
Vocabulary	Employment

Warm-Up Listening

4つの英文を聞いてイラストに最も合っているものを選びましょう。その後で、正解の文を書いてみましょう。

CheckLink DL 058 CD2-02

Ⓐ Ⓑ Ⓒ Ⓓ   Kai _____.

Word Check

次の英語の意味に合う日本語を選びましょう。

CheckLink DL 059 CD2-03

1. confidence ( )
2. employees ( )
3. employment ( )
4. experience ( )
5. job hunting ( )

a. 雇われていること、仕事
b. 就職活動
c. 経験
d. 従業員、社員
e. 自信

Kai's Blog

上の Word Check の語句を使ってKaiのブログを完成させましょう。その後で、音声を聞いて答えを確認しましょう。

DL 060 CD2-04

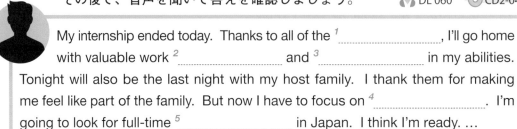

My internship ended today. Thanks to all of the ¹_____, I'll go home with valuable work ²_____ and ³_____ in my abilities. Tonight will also be the last night with my host family. I thank them for making me feel like part of the family. But now I have to focus on ⁴_____. I'm going to look for full-time ⁵_____ in Japan. I think I'm ready. ...

Conversation

A Kaiの帰国後の考えについてのWendyとの会話を聞いて順番に絵を並べましょう。

A
Job Fair

B

C

D

1. ⬜ ➡ 2. ⬜ ➡ 3. ⬜ ➡ 4. ⬜

B もう一度会話を聞いて質問に最も合う選択肢を選びましょう。

CheckLink　DL 061　CD2-05

1. How many companies will be at the job fair?

Ⓐ About 50
Ⓑ About 100
Ⓒ About 150
Ⓓ More than 200

2. When will Kai attend the job fair?

Ⓐ Tomorrow
Ⓑ In two days
Ⓒ In one week
Ⓓ In two weeks

C もう一度会話を聞いて空所を埋めましょう。　DL 061　CD2-05

Wendy: What are you going to ^{1}＿＿＿＿ after returning to Japan, Kai? Relax? Meet your friends?

Kai: No, I ^{2}＿＿＿＿ have much time for that. I have to start job hunting.

Wendy: Job hunting?

Kai: Yes, I'm going to ^{3}＿＿＿＿ a big job fair. Several hundred companies will ^{4}＿＿＿＿ there.

Wendy: Wow! So, ^{5}＿＿＿＿ have a chance to meet and talk with many recruiters.

Kai: Right. And hopefully some of the companies ^{6}＿＿＿＿ invite me for a job interview.

Wendy: So, you'll have to write a résumé, too.

Kai: Oh my gosh! Yes, a résumé. I completely forgot.

Wendy: When is the job fair?

Kai: The day after tomorrow. … HELP!

使い方のPOINT

willやbe going toは次のようなことを表す場合に使われます。後ろには動詞の原形が続きます。

will
- ①未来・予測（～でしょう、～だろう）
- ②意志（～する）

be going to
- ③予定（～する予定だ）
- ④前兆・予感（～しそうだ）
- ⑤前から決めていたこと（～するつもりだ）

①未来・予測	New employees **will** have training for one month. （新入社員は1カ月間研修を受けるでしょう） Kai **will** be satisfied with his work environment. （カイは自分の労働環境に満足するでしょう）
②意志	I **will** discuss this matter with my boss. （私はこの問題について上司と話し合います）
③予定	My sister **is going to** get a promotion to section manager. （私の姉は課長に昇進する予定です）
④前兆・予感	Wendy **is going to** work late this week. （今週、ウェンディは残業することになりそうです）
⑤前から決めていたこと	I **am going to** have an online meeting with my clients. （私はクライアントとオンラインミーティングを行います）

形　式				
will	肯定文	I/You/He/She/We/They	**will work**	in the afternoon.
	否定文	I/You/He/She/We/They	**won't work**	
	疑問文	**Will** you/he/she/they	**work**	in the afternoon**?**
be going to	肯定文	I	**am going to see**	the manager.
		You/We/They	**are going to see**	
		He/She	**is going to see**	
	否定文	I	**'m not going to see**	
		You/We/They	**aren't going to see**	
		He/She	**isn't going to see**	
	疑問文	**Am** I	**going to see**	the manager**?**
		Are you/we/they		
		Is he/she		

Take Note
- willはその場で決めたことを述べるときに使います。
  I **will** answer the phone.「私が電話に出ます」（オフィスで電話が鳴ったとき）
- be going toは前から決まっていたことを述べるときに使います。
  I **am going to** travel to England on business.「来週、私は仕事でイギリスへ行く予定です」

Grammar **Checkup**

A ( ) 内のa〜cから適当な語句を選んで文を完成させましょう。 CheckLink

1. We (a. will receive b. are going to receiving c. will be receive) our bonus soon.
2. Bob (a. be going b. is going c. will) to quit his job and start his own business.
3. A few people from the office (a. is b. are c. isn't) going to retire this year.
4. The company (a. is going to b. will go to c. will be) in the black this year.
5. Most of us (a. we'll b. will c. going to) change jobs several times in our life.
6. I'm (a. not be going to b. going to not c. not going to) work overtime today.

Notes retire「退職する」 in the black「黒字になる」 work overtime「残業する」

B 日本語を参考にして、語句を並べ替えて文を完成させましょう。
（文頭の語も小文字になっています）

1. a / bonus / receive / everyone / year-end / will （誰もが年末の賞与を受け取るでしょう）

_____.

2. a / look for / are / new job / going to / you （あなたは新しい仕事を探すつもりですか）

_____?

3. hire / new / will / the head office / workers / 200 （本社は200人の新入社員を雇うでしょう）

_____.

4. the / flextime / going / to introduce / company / isn't
（その会社はフレックスタイムを導入するつもりはありません）

_____.

C ( ) 内のa〜cから適当な語句を選んで会話を完成させましょう。その後で、音声を聞いて答えを確認しましょう。 CheckLink DL 062 ~ 063 CD2-06 ~ CD2-07

1 *At the office* （オフィスで）

A: We're going ¹(a. start b. starting c. to start) our telework system next week.
It ²(a. will b. going to c. won't) take time for everyone to learn the system.
B: Yeah, it ³(a. not going to b. won't c. will not to) be easy.

2 *In the lunchroom* （食堂で）

A: ¹(a. You'll moving b. You're going to move c. You be going to move)
into a new apartment next month, right?
B: Yes. It's near the company, so I won't ²(a. be need b. need c. to
need) to take the train anymore. I'm ³(a. going to b. go to c. will)
walk to work.

Good Reading

A テレワークに関する文章を読んで、下のa～cから適当な語句を選んで空所に書いてみましょう。その後で、音声を聞いて答えを確認しましょう。

The Future of Teleworking

Experts predict that teleworking will one day become a common way of working. Let's look at some advantages and disadvantages of teleworking. On the upside, employers [1]_____ save money on office space and electricity. Employees [2]_____ have to commute to work. These things [3]_____ lead to energy savings and less pollution.

On the downside, teleworking will reduce face-to-face professional and social communication among co-workers. This will make some workers feel isolated, lonely and unmotivated. Therefore, [4]_____ be necessary to maximize the advantages of teleworking and minimize the disadvantages.

Notes
predict「予測する」
commute「通勤（通学）する」
isolated「孤立した」
unmotivated「やる気のない」
maximize「最大にする」
minimize「最小にする」

1. a. going to   b. will   c. won't
2. a. will   b. are going to   c. won't
3. a. is going to   b. will   c. will be
4. a. it'll   b. they'll   c. we'll

B もう一度文章を読んで質問に最も合う選択肢を選びましょう。　CheckLink

1. According to the reading, what is an advantage of teleworking?

Ⓐ Lower salaries for workers
Ⓑ Fewer office costs
Ⓒ Less stress
Ⓓ More customers

2. According to the reading, what is a disadvantage of teleworking?

Ⓐ Lack of direction from the boss
Ⓑ Problems with computer equipment
Ⓒ Children making noise at home
Ⓓ Lack of direct communication with co-workers

Writing—About Me

A Kaiの例を参考にして、自分の情報を書いてみましょう。

Dream Job	Kai	You
Job title	mobile applications developer	
Location	Silicon Valley, USA	
Yearly salary	$200,000 (¥20,000,000)	
Number of employees	250-500	
Commuting time	less than 30 minutes	
Time needed for dream to come true	10 years	

B 下の動詞を使って、Kaiに関する文章を完成させましょう。

achieve   become   earn   employ   take

I'm going to ¹_____ a mobile applications developer in Silicon Valley, USA. I'll ²_____ $200,000 (¥20,000,000) a year. The company will ³_____ 250 to 500 workers. My commute will ⁴_____ less than 30 minutes. I'm going to ⁵_____ my dream in 10 years.

C **B** を参考にして、自分のことを書いてみましょう。

I'm going to _____

_____

_____

_____

Know Your Business

Grammar	比較級＆最上級
Vocabulary	**Sales & Marketing**

Warm-Up Listening

4つの英文を聞いてイラストに最も合っているものを選びましょう。その後で、正解の文を書いてみましょう。　　↻CheckLink　🎧 DL 065　◎ CD2-09

Ⓐ　Ⓑ　Ⓒ　Ⓓ _____.

Word Check

次の英語の意味に合う日本語を選びましょう。　↻CheckLink　🎧 DL 066　◎ CD2-10

1. competition 　　　　(　)
2. customer satisfaction 　(　)
3. recommend 　　　　(　)
4. reputation 　　　　(　)
5. value 　　　　　　(　)

a. 評判
b. 競争
c. 価値
d. 勧める、推薦する
e. 顧客満足

Kai's Blog

上の **Word Check** の語句を使ってKaiのブログを完成させましょう。
その後で、音声を聞いて答えを確認しましょう。　🎧 DL 067　◎ CD2-11

On my return to Japan, a passenger gave me a free business lesson. She said that [1] _____ is the best thing for any business—only satisfied customers [2] _____ a company to their friends. She also said that [3] _____ is good, and companies with the best [4] _____ always win. And [5] _____ is more important than price. … I never thought that an airplane ride could be so educational!

A 日本に帰国するKaiと同乗客の会話を聞いて順番に絵を並べましょう。

1.   ⇒   2.   ⇒   3.   ⇒   4.

B もう一度会話を聞いて質問に最も合う選択肢を選びましょう。

1. What is the woman's job?

- **A** Tour conductor
- **B** Hotel worker
- **C** Market researcher
- **D** Travel company owner

2. Why is the woman going to Japan?

- **A** To visit a friend
- **B** To eat Japanese food
- **C** To research some *ryokan*
- **D** To check out modern city hotels

C もう一度会話を聞いて空所を埋めましょう。   DL 068   CD2-12

Kai: Here, let me help you with your bag. Oh, it's ¹_____ than it looks.

Passenger: Thank you so much. Are you a college student?

Kai: Yes, I am. Are you a student, too?

Passenger: No. Actually, I own a travel agency, and Japan is one of our ²_____ popular destinations. Here's my business card.

Kai: Thank you. … Are you going to Japan on business?

Passenger: Yes. I'm going to check out some *ryokan*. Are there any in the big cities?

Kai: Yes, but they're usually ³_____ expensive than modern city hotels. *Ryokan* are more ⁴_____ in the countryside, like *minshuku*.

Passenger: What's a *minshuku*?

Kai: It's like a B&B. It's ⁵_____ than a *ryokan* and has ⁶_____ food.

Passenger: You know a lot about these things.

Kai: Of course—I'm Japanese. Ha ha ha!

Note B&B = bed and breakfast「朝食付きの（小規模の）宿」

使い方のPOINT

比較級と最上級は次のようなことを表す場合に用いられます。

比較級 あるものと他のものを比べて違いを示す

最上級 いくつかのものの中でひとつのものの違いを示す

比較級	Prices are **higher** than they were in August last year. （価格は昨年の８月より高いです） This year's marketing campaign was **more successful** than last year's. （今年のマーケティングキャンペーンは昨年のものより成功しました） Our company sold **more** cars than our main competitor. （私たちの会社はいちばんのライバル企業よりも多くの車を販売しました）
最上級	Our company had **the highest** profits last month. （先月、私たちの会社は最も高い収益をあげました） The manager showed us **the newest** marketing strategy. （部長は最新のマーケティング戦略を私たちに示しました） This is one of **the most popular** products in this shop. （これはこの店で最も人気のある製品のひとつです）

形　式		
比較級	短い形容詞→形容詞＋er	small → small**er**　rich → rich**er**
	短い副詞→副詞＋er	fast → fast**er**　hard → hard**er**
	-e → -er	nice → nic**er**　large → larg**er**
	-y → -ier	happy → happ**ier**　easy → eas**ier**
	-t/g → -tter/-gger	hot → ho**tter**　big → bi**gger**
	長い形容詞→ more ＋形容詞	beautiful → **more** beautiful
	長い副詞→ more ＋副詞	carefully → **more** carefully
	形が変わるもの	good → **better**　bad → **worse**
最上級	短い形容詞→ the ＋形容詞＋ est	small → **the** small**est**　rich → **the** rich**est**
	短い副詞→ the ＋副詞＋ est	fast → **the** fast**est**　hard → **the** hard**est**
	-e → the ＋ -est	nice → **the** nic**est**　large → **the** larg**est**
	-y → the ＋ -iest	happy → **the** happ**iest**　easy → **the** eas**iest**
	-t/g → the ＋ -ttest/ggest	hot → **the** ho**ttest**　big → **the** bi**ggest**
	長い形容詞→ the ＋ most ＋形容詞	beautiful → **the most** beautiful
	長い副詞→ the ＋ most ＋副詞	carefully → **the most** carefully
	形が変わるもの	good → **best**　bad → **worst**

Take Note
- manyとmuchの比較級と最上級は次のような形になります。
  比較級：many→**more**　much→**more**　最上級：many→**most**　much→**most**
- 数えられる「少ない」のfewと、数えられない「少ない」のlittleは次のような形になります。
  比較級：few→**fewer**　little→**less**　最上級：few→**fewest**　little→**least**

Grammar **Checkup**

A ( ) 内のa～cから適当な語句を選んで文を完成させましょう。 CheckLink

1. The company's prices are (a. low b. lower c. more lower) than its rivals.

2. This is the (a. cheap b. cheapest c. more cheapest) way to promote our brand.

3. Which is (a. more b. most c. the most) important, price or quality?

4. These are our (a. most new b. most newest than c. newest) products.

5. Men usually shop (a. quickly b. more quickly c. more quick) than women.

6. Tweeting is one of (a. best way b. the best way c. the best ways) to advertise.

B 日本語を参考にして、語句を並べ替えて文を完成させましょう。
（文頭の語も小文字になっています）

1. the / older people / customers / loyal / are / most （高齢者が最も忠実なお客様です）

   _____.

2. smaller / budget / this year's / is / than / marketing
   （今年のマーケティングの予算は昨年のものよりも少ないです）

   _____ last year's.

3. has / market share / the / maker / soft drink / largest
   （どの清涼飲料メーカーが最大の市場シェアを持っていますか）

   Which _____?

4. may / way / best / word of mouth / the / be
   （口コミがビジネスを成長させる最良の方法かもしれません）

   _____ to grow your business.

C ( ) 内のa～cから適当な語句を選んで会話を完成させましょう。その後で、音声
を聞いて答えを確認しましょう。 CheckLink DL 069 ~ 070   CD2-13 ~ CD2-14

1 *In the sales department* （営業部で）

> **A:** Our new sales manager is doing a [1](a. good b. better c. more better)
> job than our old one.
> **B:** Yes. She's [2](a. younger b. more young c. more younger) and [3](a. less
> than b. lesser than c. less) experienced, but she's a quick learner.

2 *In the marketing department* （マーケティング部で）

> **A:** Color brochures are [1](a. much b. more c. the most) attractive than black
> and white ones. But they're also more [2](a. cost b. high c. expensive).
> **B:** Let's ask the printer for a [3](a. more big b. bigger c. bigger than) discount.

Good Reading

CheckLink   DL 071   CD2-15

A KFCに関する文章を読んで、下のa〜cから適当な語句を選んで空所に書いてみましょう。その後で、音声を聞いて答えを確認しましょう。

Lost in Translation

"It's finger lickin' good," one of the most ¹_____ slogans in advertising, belongs to KFC. In 1987, KFC entered the Chinese market and used the same slogan. Unfortunately, however, the restaurant mistranslated it into Mandarin as "Eat your fingers off." Oops! Fortunately, Chinese people were more ²_____ in the chicken than they were in the slogan. KFC corrected the translation and people bought up buckets of the chicken and licked their fingers. Today, KFC is the most ³_____ fast-food chain in China. And China has the ⁴_____ KFC market in the world, with more than 5,000 restaurants—about 1,000 more than in the United States.

Notes finger lickin' good「指までなめたくなるほどおいしい」 mistranslate「誤訳する」 Mandarin「(標準) 中国語」

1.	a. succeed	b. success	c. successful
2.	a. interest	b. interested	c. interesting
3.	a. popular	b. cheap	c. favorite
4.	a. highest	b. most	c. largest

B もう一度文章を読んで質問に最も合う選択肢を選びましょう。   CheckLink

1. What was KFC's mistake in China?

- **A** It used a different name.
- **B** It entered the market too soon.
- **C** It incorrectly translated its slogan.
- **D** It used a different chicken recipe.

2. About how many KFC restaurants are there in the United States?

- **A** 1,000
- **B** 4,000
- **C** 5,000
- **D** 6,000

Writing—About Me

A Kaiが宿泊したホテルに付けた評価のように、行ったことのある2つのレストランを顔文字（☺ ☻ ☹）で評価してみましょう。

Kai				You		
Hotel	StarGaze	Sunrise	**Restaurant**			
Room rates	☺	☻	Price *(expensive)*			
Location	☹	☺	Food quality *(good)*			
Room quality	☺	☻	Service *(fast)*			
Room size	☻	☹	Atmosphere *(pleasant)*			

B 下の形容詞を正しい形に変えて、Kaiに関する文章を完成させましょう。

big   clean   comfortable   convenient   high

Kai stayed at the StarGaze Hotel and the Sunrise Hotel. The room rates at the Sunrise were ¹_____ than the room rates at the StarGaze, but the Sunrise was in a ²_____ location. The rooms were ³_____, ⁴_____, and ⁵_____ at the StarGaze. Winner: StarGaze

C **B** を参考にして、自分のことを書いてみましょう。 **A** の（　）内の形容詞を比較級にして使いましょう。

I went to two restaurants: _____ and _____.

_____

_____

_____

_____ Winner: _____

Hints   fast-food restaurants   coffee shops   family restaurants

The Job Interview

Grammar	現在完了
Vocabulary	**Job interview**

Warm-Up Listening

4つの英文を聞いてイラストに最も合っているものを選びましょう。その後で、正解の文を書いてみましょう。

↻CheckLink 🎧 DL 072 ◎CD2-16

Ⓐ Ⓑ Ⓒ Ⓓ _____ .

Word Check

次の英語の意味に合う日本語を選びましょう。

↻CheckLink 🎧 DL 073 ◎CD2-17

1. accepted　　　　(　)
2. applied　　　　 (　)
3. arranged　　　 (　)
4. contacted　　　(　)
5. offered　　　　 (　)

a. 手配した
b. 申し込んだ
c. 連絡した
d. 受け入れた
e. 申し出た

Kai's Blog

上の Word Check の語句を使ってKaiのブログを完成させましょう。その後で、音声を聞いて答えを確認しましょう。　🎧 DL 074 ◎CD2-18

Last week I ¹_____ for a job at an international IT company. The company has invited me for an interview, and I've ²_____. Their workplace language is English … and the interview will also be in English. SHOCK! After hearing this, I quickly ³_____ Linda, my internship colleague. She has kindly ⁴_____ to help me with my interview. We have ⁵_____ a Skype talk later today.

Conversation

CheckLink DL 075 CD2-19

A KaiとLindaの模擬面接の一部を聞いて順番に絵を並べましょう。

A  **B**  **C**  **D**

1. _____ ➡ 2. _____ ➡ 3. _____ ➡ 4. _____

B もう一度会話を聞いて質問に最も合う選択肢を選びましょう。

CheckLink DL 075 CD2-19

1. How long has Kai had an interest in developing mobile apps?

- **A** About two years
- **B** Three or four years
- **C** About seven years
- **D** More than ten years

2. What did Kai gain from his internship experience?

- **A** Confidence
- **B** Leadership skills
- **C** Team spirit
- **D** Creativity

C もう一度会話を聞いて空所を埋めましょう。 DL 075 CD2-19

Linda: OK, Kai, let's start. Sit up straight. … Here we go.
Thank you for coming today, Mr. Suzuki.

Kai: Thank you for inviting me. [1] _____ looked forward to meeting you.

Linda: Why have you [2] _____ for the position in our mobile app department?

Kai: I've [3] _____ interested in mobile app development [4] _____
several years. In fact, I've recently returned from a six-week internship at a
mobile app company in Silicon Valley.

Linda: How has your internship helped you?

Kai: I've [5] _____ a lot of valuable knowledge and experience by working
with IT professionals. And because of that, I've [6] _____ more
confident in my abilities and more motivated.

Linda: Wow! Kai, those were very impressive answers. Now, turn over your cheat
notes, and let's try again.

Note cheat notes「カンニングペーパー」

The Job Interview **Unit 11** | 73

Grammar Menu

使い方のPOINT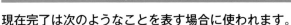

現在完了は次のようなことを表す場合に使われます。
- ①結果・完了（〜してしまった、やっと〜した［やり遂げたという気持ち］）
- ②続いている状況（ずっと〜している）
- ③現在までの経験（〜したことがある）

①結果・完了 ＊一緒によく使われる 語句：already / yet	Kai **has found** a new job.（カイはやっと新しい仕事を見つけました） I**'ve** already **had** six job interviews. （私はすでに6回面接を受けました） Kai **hasn't filled out** his job application form yet. （カイはまだエントリーシートの記入が終わっていません） **Has** Kai **finished** his work yet?（カイはもう仕事を終えましたか）
②続いている状況 ＊一緒によく使われる 語句：for / since	Kai **has had** job interviews every day for a week. （カイは1週間、毎日面接が入っています） Kai **has been job hunting** since last month. （カイは先月から就職活動をしています）
③現在までの経験 ＊一緒によく使われる 語句：ever / never	**Have** you ever **attended** a job fair? （あなたは就職説明会に参加したことがありますか） I **have** never **had** a job interview. （私は今まで一度も面接を受けたことがありません）

形　式

肯定文	I/You/We/They	**have found**	the interview room.
	He/She	**has found**	
否定文	I/You/We/They	**haven't found**	
	He/She	**hasn't found**	
疑問文	**Have** you/we/they	**found**	the interview room**?**
	Has he/she		

Take Note

- 現在完了と過去時制の違い

  I have lost my key.（私はカギをなくしてしまいました）
  → 今もないというニュアンス（今も探していて見つかることを望んでいる）

  I lost my key.（私はカギをなくしました）
  → 今もないというニュアンスはない（今は見つかって持っている可能性がある）

- 現在完了は過去を示す語句と一緒に使うことはできません。

  × I have started my own job yesterday.（私は昨日、自分の仕事を始めたところです）
  ○ I started my own job yesterday.（私は昨日、自分の仕事を始めました）

- just now（ちょうど今）は過去形と、just（ちょうど）は現在完了と一緒に使います。

  I finished my job just now.（私は自分の仕事をちょうど今、終えました）
  I've just finished my job.（私は自分の仕事をちょうど終えたところです）

Grammar **Checkup**

A (　　) 内のa〜cから適当な語句を選んで文を完成させましょう。　　CheckLink

1. Fred (a. is have b. has had c. was had) three interviews this week.

2. What (a. are you b. you've c. have you) learned about our business?

3. (a. I've always be b. I've always been c. I'm always been) a hard worker.

4. (a. Have you ever b. Have your ever c. Have you're ever) worked in sales?

5. Only one person (a. has b. have c. haven't) applied for the job.

6. (a. I ever have b. I've ever c. I've) made a portfolio before.

Note portfolio「ポートフォリオ、作品集」

B 日本語を参考にして、語句を並べ替えて文を完成させましょう。
（文頭の語も小文字になっています）

1. résumé / Ann / yet / has / her / written （Annは履歴書をもう書きましたか）

_____?

2. the / research / IT business / done / on / I've （私はITビジネスについて調べました）

_____.

3. have / interviews / started / some / online / companies
（いくつかの企業はオンライン面接を始めています）

_____.

4. sent / for a second interview / has / the personnel department / me / an invitation
（人事部は2次面接への案内を私に送りました）

_____.

C (　　) 内のa〜cから適当な語句を選んで会話を完成させましょう。その後で、音声を聞いて答えを確認しましょう。　CheckLink　DL 076 ~ 077　CD2-20 ~ CD2-21

1 *In the human resources department* （人事部で）

A: [1](a. Are b. Have c. Has) many people applied for the position?
B: Yes, [2](a. we've received b. we're receiving c. we're received) 20 applications. I've [3](a. yet b. soon c. already) scheduled some interviews.

2 *Two friends talking* （友人どうしの会話）

A: Have you [1](a. prepared b. ready c. already) for your job interview?
B: I [2](a. haven't have b. hadn't have c. haven't had) time. [3](a. I'm being b. I've been c. I've had) too busy.

Good Reading

A 就職面接に関する文章を読んで、下のa～cから適当な語句を選んで空所に書いてみましょう。その後で、音声を聞いて答えを確認しましょう。

Getting Ready for an Important Job Interview

Imagine that you have applied for a full-time job, and you have ¹_____ an invitation from the company for an interview. You REALLY want the job. But are you ready for the interview? ²_____ done everything you need to do before the big day? The checklist below will help you find out.

I have …

☐ researched the company
☐ prepared answers to common questions
☐ prepared questions for the interviewers
☐ double-checked the day, time and location of the interview

☐ ³_____ extra copies of my résumé
☐ practiced my interview with someone or in front of a mirror
☐ ⁴_____ the clothes for my interview

1. a. get	**b.** received	**c.** written
2. a. Are you	**b.** Did you	**c.** Have you
3. a. bring	**b.** made	**c.** took
4. a. chosen	**b.** choice	**c.** chose

B もう一度文章を読んで質問に最も合う選択肢を選びましょう。   CheckLink

1. What does "big day" in line 6 refer to?

- Ⓐ The date of the job application
- Ⓑ The day of the interview
- Ⓒ The day of the job offer
- Ⓓ The first day on the job

2. What should an applicant bring to a job interview?

- Ⓐ A copy of the invitation
- Ⓑ The application form
- Ⓒ A business bag
- Ⓓ Résumé copies

Note refer to …「…について言う」

Writing—About Me

A Kaiの就職面接用のメモを参考にして、自分の情報を書いてみましょう。

Q1. What have you always wanted to do?	
Kai	travel around Japan by bicycle
You	

Q2. Who has inspired you? In what way has this person inspired you?	
Kai	Professor Ito (IT professor)——motivation to work hard and never give up
You	

Q3. What is the most valuable thing you've ever experienced? What have you learned from it?	
Kai	internship in Silicon Valley——teamwork, communication
You	

Note inspire「刺激を与える」

B 下の動詞を正しい形に変えて、Kaiに関する文章を完成させましょう。

> do　dream　give　motivate　teach

- Kai has always ¹_____ of traveling around Japan by bicycle.
- Professor Ito, his IT professor, has ²_____ him inspiration. He has ³_____ him to work hard and to never give up.
- His internship in Silicon Valley is the most valuable thing he has ever ⁴_____. It has ⁵_____ him the importance of teamwork and good communication.

C **B** を参考にして、自分のことを書いてみましょう。

- I have always dreamed of _____
  _____
- _____ me inspiration.
  _____
- _____ is the most valuable thing I
  _____. _____

Is Your Company Right for You?

| Grammar | 接続詞 |
| Vocabulary | **Company culture** |

Warm-Up Listening

4つの英文を聞いてイラストに最も合っているものを選びましょう。その後で、正解の文を書いてみましょう。　CheckLink　DL 079　CD2-23

Ⓐ　Ⓑ　Ⓒ　Ⓓ　_____.

Word Check

次の英語の意味に合う日本語を選びましょう。　CheckLink　DL 080　CD2-24

1. critical （　）   **a.** 革新、刷新
2. industry （　）   **b.** 産業
3. innovation （　）   **c.** 無責任な
4. irresponsible （　）   **d.** 責任
5. responsibility （　）   **e.** 欠かせない、絶対必要な

Kai's Blog

上の Word Check の語句を使ってKaiのブログを完成させましょう。その後で、音声を聞いて答えを確認しましょう。　DL 081　CD2-25

Today was my first day at TechIzUs. My new manager Sam explained to me the company culture. The IT ¹_____ is very competitive, so ²_____ is not just important—it's ³_____. However, the company strongly believes in social ⁴_____. Developing new products is ⁵_____ if they are harmful to society or the environment. Sam also talked about the importance of making mistakes. I'm glad he feels that way. …

Conversation

CheckLink 🎧 DL 082 ◎ CD2-26

A Kaiとマネージャーの Sam の初めての打ち合わせを聞いて順番に絵を並べましょう。

1. ____ ➡ 2. ____ ➡ 3. ____ ➡ 4. ____

B もう一度会話を聞いて質問に最も合う選択肢を選びましょう。

CheckLink 🎧 DL 082 ◎ CD2-26

1. According to the manager, what is one key to success?

  A Ability

  B Passion

  C Motivation

  D Positive thinking

2. What does the manager tell Kai NOT to do?

  A Ask others for help

  B Be late for meetings

  C Eat at his desk

  D Repeat a mistake

C もう一度会話を聞いて空所を埋めましょう。　🎧 DL 082 ◎ CD2-26

Sam: [1] _____ we start our meeting, Kai, welcome to TechIzUs.

Kai: Thank you for hiring me and for giving me this opportunity.

Sam: We hired you [2] _____ we think you'll be a good fit for the company.

Kai: I look forward to meeting everyone [3] _____ working with them.

Sam: We have a great staff. We all support each other.

Kai: I'm sure I'll need all the support I can get.

Sam: Don't worry. You'll do fine, Kai. And don't be afraid to make mistakes. People learn the most [4] _____ they make mistakes. You'll be successful [5] _____ you have passion for your job and work hard.

Kai: I do have passion for my job, and I hardly work. … Wait, that was a mistake. I mean, I work hard. Sorry.

Sam: Ha ha ha! That's OK, [6] _____ just don't make the same mistake twice.

Note be a good fit「ぴったりである」

接続詞には「文と文」や「句と句」を結びつける働きがあります。

対等の文や句を結びつけるもの（等位接続詞）

① ～ and …「～そして…」/ ～ but …「～しかし…」 ＊文と文、句と句が結びつく

② ～ or …「～または（あるいは）…」 ＊文と文、句と句が結びつく

③ ～, so …「～だから…（～なので…）」 ＊文と文が結びつく

補助する文を結びつけるもの（従属接続詞）

④ ～ before …「…する前に～」/ ～ after …「…する後に～」

⑤ ～ although …「…だけれども～」

⑥ ～ because …「…なので～ / ～、だから…」

⑦ ～ if …「もし…なら～」/ ～ unless …「もし…ではないなら～」

⑧ ～ when …「…するとき～」

① and/but	Our company cares about the environment **and** makes eco-friendly products. （私たちの会社は環境に配慮し、環境にやさしい製品を作ります） Good teamwork **and** communication are critical to our company. （よいチームワークとコミュニケーションは私たちの会社にとって欠かせません） My boss points out my mistakes, **but** he doesn't scold me. （私の上司はミスは指摘しますが、しかりはしません） Kai is inexperienced **but** highly motivated. （カイは未経験ですが、とてもやる気があります）
② or	Employees can work from home **or** go to work by car. （社員は自宅で勤務するか車で通勤するか選ぶことができます） We have a meeting with our section chief **or** manager once a week. （私たちは課長か部長と週に1回ミーティングを行います）
③ so	Your colleagues are very kind, **so** please don't worry. （同僚たちはとても親切なので、心配しないでください）
④ before/ after	We always double-check our documents **before** we give them to our boss. （私たちは上司に渡す前に、いつも書類を再確認します） Our work environment improved **after** the new CEO took over. （新しいCEOが引き継いでから、私たちの労働環境は改善されました）
⑤ although	Kai is already working on a big project **although** he is a new staff member. （カイは新入社員ですが、すでに大きなプロジェクトに取り組んでいます）
⑥ because	Sam will take paid leave **because** he thinks work-life balance is important. （サムは仕事と人生のバランスが大切だと考えているので、有給休暇を取ります）
⑦ if/unless	You can talk to human resources **if** you have any trouble. （従業員は困ったことがあれば、人事部に相談することができます） The company picnic will take place **unless** it rains. （雨が降らないかぎり、会社の野外親睦会は行われます）
⑧ when	Employees can take time off **when** they have a baby. （従業員は子どもが生まれるときに、休みを取ることができます）

Take Note
● 従属接続詞で文が始まる場合はカンマ（,）が必要です。
Because he thinks work-life balance is important, Sam will take paid leave.

Grammar **Checkup**

A (   ) 内のa～cから適当な語句を選んで文を完成させましょう。　　🔄 CheckLink

1. Which do you prefer, working alone (**a.** and　**b.** but　**c.** or) working on a team?

2. Mike's company has a friendly (**a.** and　**b.** but　**c.** so) relaxed atmosphere.

3. Mary didn't get along with her boss, (**a.** because　**b.** so　**c.** but) she quit.

4. (**a.** Although　**b.** If　**c.** When) the manager often gets angry, the staff likes her.

5. Workers lose motivation (**a.** so　**b.** when　**c.** before) their work isn't challenging.

6. We will fail (**a.** because　**b.** but　**c.** unless) we change our management style.

B 日本語を参考にして、語句を並べ替えて文を完成させましょう。
（文頭の語も小文字になっています）

1. but / is / supervisor / fair / my / strict （私の上司は厳しいけれども公平です）

_____ .

2. expectations / has / and / the president / demands / unrealistic
（社長は現実的でない要求と期待を抱いています）

_____ .

3. you're / here / succeed / you'll / ambitious / if
（あなたが野心的であれば、あなたはここで成功するでしょう）

_____ .

4. new management / motivation / took over / staff / after / improved
（新しい経営者が引き継いでから、スタッフのやる気は向上しました）

_____ .

C (   ) 内のa～cから適当な語句を選んで会話を完成させましょう。その後で、音声
を聞いて答えを確認しましょう。　🔄 CheckLink　⬇ DL 083 ~ 084　◉ CD2-27 ~ ◉ CD2-28

1 *Two friends talking* （友人どうしの会話）

A: How do you like your new job?
B: I like it [1](**a.** because　**b.** so　**c.** after) the work is challenging. My
colleagues are all busy, [2](**a.** and　**b.** but　**c.** or) they are very helpful. And
my boss doesn't get angry [3](**a.** so　**b.** before　**c.** when) I make mistakes.

2 *Employee to new staffer* （社員から新しいスタッフへ）

A: The work is fast-paced, [1](**a.** because　**b.** but　**c.** so) it will keep you busy.
[2](**a.** Before　**b.** If　**c.** Unless) you have any questions, feel free to ask me.
B: Thank you for your support [3](**a.** after　**b.** and　**c.** or) encouragement.

Note encouragement「励まし」

Good Reading

CheckLink DL 085 CD2-29

A 企業文化・社風に関する文章を読んで、下のa〜cから適当な語句を選んで空所に書いてみましょう。その後で、音声を聞いて答えを確認しましょう。

Fitting in with the Company Culture

Company culture is basically the personality of a company. It includes such things as work environment, values, expectations and goals. Employees are more likely to enjoy their work ¹ ＿＿＿＿＿＿＿ they fit in with the company culture. They develop good relationships with co-workers, and are motivated and productive. However, if you like working alone, ² ＿＿＿＿＿＿＿ your company emphasizes teamwork, you probably won't enjoy your job ³ ＿＿＿＿＿＿＿ do your best work. So ⁴ ＿＿＿＿＿＿＿ you accept any job offer, make sure that you and the company culture are a good fit.

Notes basically「基本的に」 personality「個性、性格」 productive「生産的な」 emphasize「強調する」

1.	a. when	b. unless	c. so
2.	a. so	b. or	c. but
3.	a. if	b. but	c. or
4.	a. after	b. before	c. because

B もう一度文章を読んで質問に最も合う選択肢を選びましょう。　CheckLink

1. What is another way to describe company culture?

Ⓐ Company character
Ⓑ Company history
Ⓒ Company tradition
Ⓓ Company rules

2. What is the writer's advice to job hunters?

Ⓐ Apply for jobs with a company culture.
Ⓑ Learn to work well on a team.
Ⓒ Don't accept a job offer until you understand the company culture.
Ⓓ Learn about the company culture after you join the company.

Writing—About Me

A Kaiの例を参考にして、自分の情報を書いてみましょう。

Kai

I'm ☑ outgoing ☐ shy ☑ positive ☑ stubborn ☑ serious. *Other:* ambitious

A ☐ small company ☑ big company is best for me.
Reason: can meet new people; more opportunities for advancement

I like working ☐ alone ☑ on a team. *Reason:* can develop a better product

I prefer ☑ face-to-face ☐ email communication. *Reason:* like immediate feedback

Notes outgoing「社交的な」 stubborn「頑固な」 advancement「進歩、出世」 immediate「即座の」 feedback「反応、意見」

You

I'm ☐ outgoing ☐ shy ☐ positive ☐ stubborn ☐ serious. *Other:* _____

☐ Small classes ☐ Big classes are best for me. *Reason:* _____

I like working ☐ alone ☐ in a group. *Reason:* _____

I prefer ☐ face-to-face ☐ email communication. *Reason:* _____

B 下の接続詞を使って、Kaiに関する文章を完成させましょう。

and   because   but   if   so

Kai is outgoing, positive, serious ¹_____ ambitious, ²_____ also stubborn. A big company is best for him ³_____ he can meet new people, and he has more opportunities for advancement. He thinks he can develop a better product ⁴_____ he works on a team. He likes immediate feedback, ⁵_____ he prefers face-to-face communication.

C **B** を参考にして、自分のことを書いてみましょう。

I'm _____.
_____ classes are best for me because _____
_____. I think I can _____
_____ when I work_____. _____
_____, so I prefer _____ communication.

Hints · participate in class discussions   · work/learn faster/better   · ask questions

Email Matters

Grammar	動名詞&不定詞
Vocabulary	**Email**

Warm-Up Listening

4つの英文を聞いてイラストに最も合っているものを選びましょう。その後で、正解の文を書いてみましょう。　⟳CheckLink　🎧 DL 086　◉ CD2-30

kaimono640
kaisuzu@zuki.com

Ⓐ　Ⓑ　Ⓒ　Ⓓ ＿＿＿＿＿＿＿＿＿＿＿＿＿＿＿＿＿＿ .

Word Check

次の英語の意味に合う日本語を選びましょう。　⟳CheckLink　🎧 DL 087　◉ CD2-31

1. complaints	( )		**a.**	効果的な
2. confusion	( )		**b.**	不満、苦情
3. effective	( )		**c.**	あいまいな
4. technical	( )		**d.**	専門的な
5. vague	( )		**e.**	混乱

Kai's Blog

上の Word Check の語句を使って Kai のブログを完成させましょう。
その後で、音声を聞いて答えを確認しましょう。　🎧 DL 088　◉ CD2-32

As part of my training at TechIzUs, I'm learning to write [1]＿＿＿＿＿＿＿＿＿ emails in English. My colleague Hana is helping me with that. She says that emails need to be clear, not [2]＿＿＿＿＿＿＿＿＿. But she also told me to avoid using [3]＿＿＿＿＿＿＿ words with customers. It may cause misunderstandings or [4]＿＿＿＿＿＿＿, and we don't want to hear any [5]＿＿＿＿＿＿＿＿＿ from customers. Hana always says, "simple is best."

Conversation

A Kaiと同僚のHanaの新プロジェクトに関する会話を聞いて順番に絵を並べましょう。

1. ➡ 2. ➡ 3. ➡ 4.

B もう一度会話を聞いて質問に最も合う選択肢を選びましょう。

CheckLink · DL 089 · CD2-33

1. When did Sam send the email?

- **A** Last night
- **B** A few minutes ago
- **C** About 30 minutes ago
- **D** Two or three hours ago

2. What does the company sell?

- **A** Fresh fruit and vegetables
- **B** Ready-made dishes
- **C** Bread and cakes
- **D** Bottled water and soft drinks

C もう一度会話を聞いて空所を埋めましょう。 DL 089 · CD2-33

Hana: Excuse me, Kai. Did you read Sam's email to us?

Kai: No, I haven't finished ¹＿＿＿＿＿＿＿ my email yet. What does it say?

Hana: He wants you and me ²＿＿＿＿＿＿＿ a mobile app for a food delivery company.

Kai: Oh, good. … Well, there's nothing in my inbox from Sam. When did he send it?

Hana: About half an hour ago. Should I ask him ³＿＿＿＿＿＿＿ it?

Kai: I think he's in a meeting now. Would you mind ⁴＿＿＿＿＿＿＿ it to me?

Hana: Sure. … I'm sending it now.

Kai: … Ah, here it is. Thanks. … Wow! What a coincidence. I started ⁵＿＿＿＿＿＿＿ food from this company a couple of months ago.

Hana: You did?

Kai: Yeah, they sell all kinds of pre-cooked meals. All you need ⁶＿＿＿＿＿＿＿ is heat them up in the microwave.

Hana: Well, like I always say, "simple is best."

Notes inbox「受信トレイ」 What a coincidence.「何て偶然なんだ」

Grammar Menu

使い方のPOINT

動詞の後ろには「動名詞 (-ing)」や「不定詞 (to＋動詞の原形)」が来ることがあります。動詞によって次の3つのタイプに分かれます。

①動詞＋動名詞：admit, avoid, consider, enjoy, finish, mind, practice, recommend, suggest など

②動詞＋不定詞：agree, appear, ask, choose, decide, expect, hope, learn, need, offer, promise, refuse, seem, wait, want など

③動詞＋動名詞または不定詞：begin, continue, forget, hate, like, love, prefer, remember, start など

①動詞＋動名詞	Kai **enjoys chatting** with his foreign friends. （カイは外国人の友人たちとチャットを楽しんでいます） Kai **finished sending** his résumé by email. （カイはメールで履歴書を送り終えました） Kai **practices writing** business emails in English. （カイは英語でビジネスEメールを書く練習をしています） We **recommend following** business email etiquette rules. （私たちはビジネスEメールのエチケットに従うことを勧めます） Would you **mind giving** me your email address? （メールアドレスを教えてもらってもいいですか）
②動詞＋不定詞	We **agreed to keep** in touch by email. （私たちはEメールで連絡を取り合うことに同意しました） Kai **promised to reply** to his client as soon as possible. （カイは顧客にできるだけ早く返信することを約束しました） Hana **refuses to give** her personal information by email. （ハナはEメールで個人情報を提供することを拒否します）
③動詞＋動名詞または不定詞	Hana **loves receiving/loves to receive** emails from her old friends. （ハナは昔の友人からEメールをもらうのが大好きです） Kai **prefers working/prefers to work** face-to-face. （カイは直接会って仕事をするほうが好きです） We will **continue contacting/continue to contact** consumers by email. （私たちは引き続き消費者にEメールで連絡を取ります）

Take Note

● 後ろに動名詞または不定詞が来る動詞の中には、forgetやrememberのように意味が変わるものがあります。一般的に、動名詞は過去のことを示し、不定詞はこれから起こることを示します。

I'll never **forget receiving** that important email from the company.
（その会社から重要なEメールをもらったことを決して忘れないでしょう）

Don't **forget to send** the attachment.
（添付書類を送るのを忘れてはいけません）

Kai **remembers receiving** the customer's reply.
（カイは顧客からの返信を受け取ったことを覚えています）

Remember to check your email before you go home.
（家に帰る前にEメールを確認するのを覚えておいてください）

Grammar **Checkup**

A ( ) 内のa〜cから適当な語句を選んで文を完成させましょう。　　○CheckLink

1. I'll email you my report after I finish (**a.** to check　**b.** checking　**c.** a または b) it.

2. Everyone hates (**a.** to get　**b.** getting　**c.** a または b) urgent email late in the day.

3. Joe decided (**a.** to email　**b.** emailing　**c.** a または b) his manager about his concerns.

4. Emma enjoys (**a.** to receive　**b.** receiving　**c.** a または b) E-cards from her friends.

5. We're expecting (**a.** to hear　**b.** hearing　**c.** a または b) from the head office today.

6. I recommend (**a.** to forward　**b.** forwarding　**c.** a または b) the complaint to your manager.

Notes urgent「緊急の」　concern「心配事」

B 日本語を参考にして、語句を並べ替えて文を完成させましょう。
（文頭の語も小文字になっています）

1. be / the / down / server / to / seems （サーバーがダウンしているようです）

   _____ .

2. to / my / like / email / check / I （私はEメールを頻ぱんに確認するのが好きです）

   _____ frequently.

3. junk mail / getting / of / I've / lots / started （私は多くの迷惑メールをもらい始めました）

   _____ .

4. his / cc / Tom / boss / to / forgot （トムは上司にCCするのを忘れました）

   _____ .

C ( ) 内のa〜cから適当な語句を選んで会話を完成させましょう。その後で、音声
を聞いて答えを確認しましょう。　○CheckLink　🎧 DL 090〜091　◎CD2-34 〜 ◎CD2-35

1 *In the accounting department* （経理部で）

> **A:** We're still waiting [1](**a.** to receive　**b.** receiving　**c.** to receiving) payment from
> a customer. He promised [2](**a.** to payment　**b.** to paid　**c.** to pay) by June 1.
> **B:** I suggest [3](**a.** to send　**b.** sending　**c.** to sent) him a reminder.

Note reminder「思い出させるもの、リマインダー」

2 *Two co-workers talking* （同僚どうしの会話）

> **A:** Do you prefer [1](**a.** email　**b.** emailing　**c.** to emailing) co-workers in other
> departments or [2](**a.** telephone them　**b.** speak with them on the phone
> **c.** contacting them by telephone)?
> **B:** If I need [3](**a.** know　**b.** to know　**c.** knowing) something right away, I call them.

Good Reading

A ネチケットに関する文章を読んで、下のa～cから適当な語句を選んで空所に書いてみましょう。その後で、音声を聞いて答えを確認しましょう。

Netiquette

To maintain a good and trusting relationship with customers, follow these four Internet etiquette, or "netiquette," rules.

Rule 1: Make sure the correct name of the receiver appears in the "To" box. And don't forget [1]_____ any files you want [2]_____.

Rule 2: Keep your email short, but remember [3]_____ polite and friendly, too.

Rule 3: Avoid [4]_____ CAPITAL LETTERS. It's rude. Use *italics*, underlining, or **bold** to emphasize important points.

Rule 4: Check for spelling and grammar mistakes. If you make careless mistakes in your email, customers will think you also make careless mistakes in your work.

---

1. **a.** attach   **b.** attaching   **c.** to attach
2. **a.** to send   **b.** sending   **c.** to sending
3. **a.** being   **b.** to be   **c.** to being
4. **a.** using   **b.** to use   **c.** being used

B もう一度文章を読んで質問に最も合う選択肢を選びましょう。 CheckLink

1. What shouldn't an email sender do?

Ⓐ Write long emails
Ⓑ Send more than one attachment
Ⓒ Use bold type
Ⓓ Worry about small mistakes

2. In Rule 3, what does the word "rude" mean?

Ⓐ Unattractive
Ⓑ Unimportant
Ⓒ Impossible
Ⓓ Impolite

Writing—About Me

A Kaiの例を参考にして、自分の情報を書いてみましょう。

How many times a day do you check your email?				
Kai: ☐ 0-5 ☐ 6-10 ☐ 11-20 ☑ 20-40 ☐ more than 40				
You: ☐ 0-5 ☐ 6-10 ☐ 11-20 ☐ 20-40 ☐ more than 40				
If you email or text a friend with a question, when do you hope to get an answer?				
Kai: Within: ☐ an hour ☐ a few hours ☐ a day ☑ a few days ☐ a week				
You: Within: ☐ an hour ☐ a few hours ☐ a day ☐ a few days ☐ a week				
Your inbox has some unopened email. Which one do you look at and reply to first?				
The one from …				
Kai: ☐ my best friend ☑ my boss ☐ a family member ☐ *Other:* _____				
You: ☐ my best friend ☐ my boss ☐ a family member ☐ *Other:* _____				
What kind of emails do you usually not open?				
Emails from …				
Kai: ☑ unknown senders ☑ *Other:* <u>stores and restaurants</u>				
You: ☐ unknown senders ☐ *Other:* _____				

B 下の動詞を正しい形に変えて、Kaiに関する文章を完成させましょう。

> *answer   opening   to check   to read   to receive*

Kai likes ¹_____ his inbox for messages 20-40 times a day. If he emails or texts a friend with a question, he expects ²_____ a reply within a few days. When he sees some unopened email, he chooses ³_____ and ⁴_____ any from his boss first. He avoids ⁵_____ emails from unknown senders and from stores and restaurants.

C **B** を参考にして、自分のことを書いてみましょう。

I like _____ my inbox for messages _____ times a day. If I email or text a friend with a question, I _____ _____. When I see some unopened email, I _____ and _____ any from _____ first. I avoid _____.

Unit 14

On the Move

Grammar	受動態
Vocabulary	**Housing**

Warm-Up Listening

4つの英文を聞いてイラストに最も合っているものを選びましょう。その後で、正解の文を書いてみましょう。

⟲CheckLink 🎧 DL 093 ◎ CD2-37

Ⓐ Ⓑ Ⓒ Ⓓ _____.

Word Check

次の英語の意味に合う日本語を選びましょう。

⟲CheckLink 🎧 DL 094 ◎ CD2-38

1. deposit ( )
2. key money ( )
3. neighborhood ( )
4. required ( )
5. savings ( )

a. 礼金
b. 近所
c. 求められる
d. 保証金、敷金
e. 貯金

Kai's Blog

上の Word Check の語句を使って Kai のブログを完成させましょう。その後で、音声を聞いて答えを確認しましょう。 🎧 DL 095 ◎ CD2-39

Yesterday I moved into a new apartment. Before moving in, I was
¹_____ to pay a ²_____ and ³_____. I
used most of my ⁴_____, but now I have a nice apartment in a great
⁵_____. I showed Hana a photo this morning. It was taken from my
balcony.

Conversation

CheckLink　DL 096　CD2-40

A KaiがHanaに新しいアパートについて話しているのを聞いて順番に絵を並べましょう。

A　B　C　D

1. 　➡　2. 　➡　3. 　➡　4.

B もう一度会話を聞いて質問に最も合う選択肢を選びましょう。

CheckLink　DL 096　CD2-40

1. What motivated Kai to move?

Ⓐ Cheaper rent
Ⓑ Larger rooms
Ⓒ More greenery
Ⓓ A wider balcony

2. What will Kai probably get soon?

Ⓐ A pet
Ⓑ Some plants
Ⓒ Some new furniture
Ⓓ A car

C もう一度会話を聞いて空所を埋めましょう。　DL 096　CD2-40

Hana: Hey Kai, I heard that you moved into a new apartment.

Kai: That's right. My lease started today, but I ¹＿＿＿＿＿ ²＿＿＿＿＿ I could move in over the weekend.

Hana: You must have been really busy.

Kai: Yeah. I ³＿＿＿＿ ⁴＿＿＿＿ the keys on Friday evening. I packed up all my things on Saturday, and I moved in on Sunday.

Hana: That was fast. Why did you decide to move?

Kai: Well, pets ⁵＿＿＿＿ ⁶＿＿＿＿ in my old place, and I've always wanted to have a cat. And my new neighborhood has a lot more trees and flowers than my old neighborhood.

Hana: Are there some nice parks around your new apartment?

Kai: Yes. In fact, it has a balcony overlooking a park. Here's a photo.

Hana: Hey, that's not a park.

Kai: Yes, it is. It's a *car* park.

Note lease「賃貸借（契約）」

使い方のPOINT

能動態と受動態は意味としては同じ内容を表しますが、話題の焦点となるものが異なります。

能動態　John and Mary **bought** a house in Yokohama.
（ジョンとメアリーは横浜の家を買いました→焦点は「ジョンとメアリー」）

受動態　The house in Yokohama **was bought** by John and Mary.
（横浜の家はジョンとメアリーによって買われました→焦点は「横浜の家」）

そのほかに、受動態は次のようなことを表す場合に使われます。
①動作をしている人がわからない
②動作をしている人があまり重要でない
③動作を表す
④状態を表す

①動作主がわからない	Our new refrigerator **was delivered** this morning. （新しい冷蔵庫が今朝届けられました）
②動作主が重要ではない	That apartment building **was built** last year. （そのアパートは去年建てられました）
③動作を表す	Delivery lockers **are** often **used** these days. （近頃では宅配ロッカーがよく使われます）
④状態を表す	Key money **is called** "reikin" in Japanese. （Key moneyは日本語では「礼金」と呼ばれます）

形　式				
肯定文	現在形	Pets	**are allowed**	in the apartment building.
	過去形		**were allowed**	
否定文	現在形	Pets	**aren't allowed**	in the apartment building.
	過去形		**weren't allowed**	
疑問文	現在形	**Are**	pets	**allowed**	in the apartment building**?**
	過去形	**Were**			

Take Note
● by~をつけると「～によって」と誰かがそうしたことを強調し、ない場合は「その状態になっている」ということを強調します。

The house repairs were completed.（その家の修理は終えられました）

The house repairs were completed **by** a local company.
（その家の修理は地元の会社によって終えられました）

● 受動態には状態を表すものと動作を表すものがあります。動作を表す受動態では、be動詞の代わりにgetを使うこともあります。

This office was closed for three days.（このオフィスは3日間閉鎖されました）
　　→ 閉鎖された状態が3日間続いている

This office was/got opened by him.（このオフィスは彼によって開けられました）
　　→ オフィスを開くという動作が行われている

Grammar **Checkup**

A ( ) 内のa〜cから適当な語句を選んで文を完成させましょう。 　CheckLink

1. The windows of my condominium are (a. washed　b. wash　c. washing) twice a year.

2. The house (a. is own　b. is owned　c. was owning) by a well-known artist.

3. The rent (a. paid　b. was paid　c. has paid) at the beginning of the month.

4. (a. You allowed　b. Are you allow　c. Are you allowed) to smoke in your apartment?

5. Many old houses were (a. damaged　b. damages　c. damaging) in the earthquake.

6. This Beverly Hills mansion was (a. sale　b. sell　c. sold) for $20 million.

Note condominium「分譲マンション」

B 日本語を参考にして、語句を並べ替えて文を完成させましょう。
（文頭の語も小文字になっています）

1. recommended / me / corner unit / to / the / was （角部屋が私に勧められました）

_____.

2. antiques / furnished / house / with / the / is
（その家はアンティークの家具が備え付けられています）

_____.

3. two / at / installed / the entrance / are / security cameras
（2台の監視カメラが玄関に設置されています）

_____.

4. wasn't / signed / agreement / why / rental / the （なぜ賃貸契約書は署名されなかったのですか）

_____?

C ( ) 内のa〜cから適当な語句を選んで会話を完成させましょう。その後で、音声
を聞いて答えを確認しましょう。　CheckLink　　DL 097〜098　　CD2-41　〜　CD2-42

1 *At a real estate agency* （不動産店で）

A: What maintenance [1](a. was did　b. has done　c. was done) on the cottage?
B: The walls [2](a. was painted　b. were painted　c. were painting) and the roof
　[3](a. was fixed　b. has fixed　c. did fix).

2 *At an open house* （オープンハウスで）

A: This mansion was [1](a. design　b. designed　c. designer) by a famous
　architect in 1920. It [2](a. has　b. is　c. was) bought by a rich elderly couple.
B: It's beautiful.　When [3](a. was the pool added　b. the pool was added
　c. was added the pool)?

Note architect「建築家」

Good Reading

A シェアハウスに関する文章を読んで、下のa〜cから適当な語句を選んで空所に書いてみましょう。その後で、音声を聞いて答えを確認しましょう。

Share Houses

These days, a growing number of people in Japan are choosing to live in share houses. Each resident usually has their own bedroom, while the kitchen, toilet, bathroom and living areas
¹_____. In general, the houses
²_____, and the utilities (water, gas and electricity) are ³_____ in the rent. This makes them very affordable. Some people are ⁴_____ to theme-based share houses. There, they can meet people with similar interests, such as cycling, anime, or gardening. Some share houses even have daycare services for single mothers.

Notes resident「住人」 utilities「公共料金」 theme-based「テーマに基づいた」

1.	**a.** are shared	**b.** are sharing	**c.** were shared
2.	**a.** are furniture	**b.** were finished	**c.** are furnished
3.	**a.** include	**b.** included	**c.** including
4.	**a.** attractive	**b.** attraction	**c.** attracted

B もう一度文章を読んで質問に最も合う選択肢を選びましょう。 CheckLink

1. In line 8, what does the word "affordable" mean?

Ⓐ Basic
Ⓑ Casual
Ⓒ Comfortable
Ⓓ Inexpensive

2. Who probably lives in a theme-based share house?

Ⓐ People with the same hobby
Ⓑ Amusement park lovers
Ⓒ People with different interests
Ⓓ Single mothers

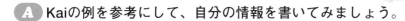

Writing—About Me

Kaiの例を参考にして、自分の情報を書いてみましょう。

	Kai	You
Your type of residence	apartment	
Location of your residence	Nakano Ward, Tokyo	
Age of residence	～ 20 years	
Nearest station	Shin-Nakano	
Area attractions	anime and manga shops	
Food recommendations	ramen, yakitori	

Notes residence「住居」 ward「区」 recommendation「おすすめ」

B 下の動詞を正しい受動態の形に変えて、Kaiに関する文章を完成させましょう。

build   call   know   locate   recommend

Kai lives in an apartment. The apartment ¹_____ in Nakano Ward, Tokyo. It ²_____ about 20 years ago. The nearest station ³_____ Shin-Nakano Station. Nakano ⁴_____ for its many anime and manga shops. Ramen and yakitori ⁵_____ for first-time visitors to the area.

C B を参考にして、自分のことを書いてみましょう。

I live in _____. The _____ in _____. It _____ ago. The nearest station _____. _____ for its _____ and _____. _____ for first-time visitors to the area.

Unit 15

Good News

Grammar 関係詞

Vocabulary Events & Experiences

Warm-Up Listening

4つの英文を聞いてイラストに最も合っているものを選びましょう。その後で、正解の文を書いてみましょう。　CheckLink　DL 100　CD2-44

Ⓐ　Ⓑ　Ⓒ　Ⓓ _____.

Word Check

次の英語の意味に合う日本語を選びましょう。　CheckLink　DL 101　CD2-45

1. announce 　（　）　　a. 機能
2. confirmed 　（　）　　b. 保護されて
3. functions 　（　）　　c. 確認した
4. protected 　（　）　　d. 安全
5. security 　（　）　　e. 発表する

Kai's Blog

上の Word Check の語句を使ってKaiのブログを完成させましょう。その後で、音声を聞いて答えを確認しましょう。　DL 102　CD2-46

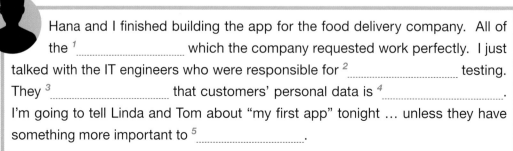

Hana and I finished building the app for the food delivery company. All of the ¹_____ which the company requested work perfectly. I just talked with the IT engineers who were responsible for ²_____ testing. They ³_____ that customers' personal data is ⁴_____. I'm going to tell Linda and Tom about "my first app" tonight … unless they have something more important to ⁵_____.

Conversation

A Kaiが Lindaと Tomと Skypeで話しているのを聞いて順番に絵を並べましょう。

 Ⓐ
 Ⓑ
 Ⓒ
 Ⓓ

1. ▢ ➡ 2. ▢ ➡ 3. ▢ ➡ 4. ▢

B もう一度会話を聞いて質問に最も合う選択肢を選びましょう。

CheckLink 🎧 DL 103 ⊙ CD2-47

1. What did Linda and Tom inspire Kai to do?

- Ⓐ Skype with them
- Ⓑ Learn English
- Ⓒ Graduate from university
- Ⓓ Build a career in IT

2. What do we learn about Linda and Tom?

- Ⓐ They changed jobs.
- Ⓑ They got married in June.
- Ⓒ They are coming to Japan.
- Ⓓ They are going to get married.

C もう一度会話を聞いて空所を埋めましょう。　🎧 DL 103 ⊙ CD2-47

Tom: It's good to see you, Kai. How's your job going?

Kai: Great. The time ¹ _____ I spent working with you and Linda was really helpful. Actually, you two are the ones ² _____ inspired me to pursue a career in IT.

Linda: Aww, that's so kind of you to say, Kai. Thank you. … Well, the reason ³ _____ we asked you to Skype with us today is to tell you that Tom and I are getting married.

Kai: Really? I had no idea. … Congratulations!

Linda: Thanks. Remember the restaurant ⁴ _____ the three of us had dinner?

Kai: Yeah, that was the time ⁵ _____ I got sick after eating that huge brownie.

Linda: Right. That's where Tom proposed to me. … Anyway, we would like you to come to our wedding, ⁶ _____ will be held in June in San Francisco.

Kai: Thank you. I'd love to attend! … But I don't know if Tina will like the idea.

Tom: I didn't know you had a girlfriend, Kai.

Kai: Well, I do. In fact, she's here with me now. … Tina, meet Linda and Tom.

Tina: Meow!

使い方のPOINT

関係詞（who / that / which / whose / when / why / where）は、それが修飾するもの（先行詞）に限定的な情報を与えたり、付加的な情報を与えたりします。付加的な情報を与える場合、関係詞の前にカンマ（,）が入ります。

限定的な情報	I know the woman **who** is making the speech. （私はスピーチをしている女性を知っています）
付加的な情報	The restaurant, **which** is located near my house, is popular among actors. （このレストラン——私の家の近くにある——は俳優たちに人気があります）

関係詞の用法

　①who/thatは「人」、②which/thatは「物」「場所」、③「whose＋名詞」は所有関係、
　④whenは「時」、⑤whyは「理由」、⑥whereは「場所」について述べます。

①who/that「人」	Kai has several friends **who** will help him prepare for the party. （カイにはパーティーの準備を手伝ってくれる何人かの友人がいます）
②which/that「物」「場所」	This is the wedding present **which/that** Kai bought for Linda and Tom. （これがリンダとトムのためにカイが買った結婚祝いのプレゼントです）
	Kai went to the café **which/that** is popular among young people. （カイは若者に人気のあるカフェに行きました）
③whose＋名詞「所有関係」	Kai met the man **whose father** is a world-famous IT professor. （カイは世界的に有名なITの教授を父に持つ男性に会いました）
	Linda and Tom bought a house **whose garden** is very beautiful. （リンダとトムはきれいな庭のある家を購入しました）
④when「時」	I remember the days **when** we studied together at university. （私は大学で私たちが一緒に勉強した日々を覚えています）
⑤why「理由」	There are several reasons **why** I like the festival. （私がそのお祭りを好きなのにはいくつかの理由があります）
⑥where「場所」	Tokyo Big Sight is a famous place **where** many events are held. （東京ビックサイトはたくさんのイベントが行われる有名な場所です）

Take Note

- 付加的な情報を与える場合、関係詞に続く部分は「その前に述べられていることへのコメント」を表します。
- 付加的な情報を与える関係詞はwhichとwhoで、thatは使われません。
- 先行詞が「人」と「人以外のもの」の両方を含む場合はthatを用います。

　Did you see the woman and the dog **that** were running across the road?
　（道路を横切っていたあの女性と犬を見ましたか）

- 先行詞が「場所」や「時」でも、動詞がvisitやspendなどの場合は関係代名詞を使います。

　Do you remember the ball park **which** we visited five years ago?
　（私たちが5年前に訪れた野球場を覚えていますか？）　＊先行詞the ball parkはvisitの目的語

　He remembered the days **which** he spent with his girlfriend.
　（彼は彼女と過ごした日々を思い出しました）　＊先行詞the daysはspendの目的語

Grammar **Checkup**

A ( ) 内のa〜cから適当な語句を選んで文を完成させましょう。　　○CheckLink

1. The business conference (a. who b. that c. when) I attended was excellent.

2. This is the place (a. which b. where c. when) we had Kai's welcome party.

3. The people (a. who b. whose c. which) organized the event were all volunteers.

4. That was the day (a. when b. where c. which) the family reunion was held.

5. The coach (a. who b. whose c. who's) team won the tournament signed a new contract.

6. The meeting, (a. that b. when c. which) starts at 3 p.m., will be held online.

Note family reunion「親族会」

B 日本語を参考にして、語句を並べ替えて文を完成させましょう。
（文頭の語も小文字になっています）

1. British / performed / the / is / who / musician （演奏した音楽家はイギリス人でした）

_____.

2. the festival / is / best / I like / this / that （これは私がいちばん好きなお祭りです）

_____.

3. I / was / awesome / saw / that / the fireworks display
（私が見た花火大会は素晴らしかったです）

_____.

4. canceled / the business trip / why / no one / knows / was
（出張が中止された理由を誰も知りませんでした）

_____.

C ( ) 内のa〜cから適当な語句を選んで会話を完成させましょう。その後で、音声を聞いて答えを確認しましょう。　　○CheckLink　🎧DL 104 ~ 105　◎CD2-48 ~ ◎CD2-49

1 *A Halloween party* （ハロウィンパーティー）

A: Is this the Halloween photo ¹(a. when b. who c. that) Jim gave you?
B: Yes. The person ²(a. who b. who's c. whose) wearing the Dracula costume is Ed. And the one ³(a. whose b. that c. which) face is green is Donna.

2 *A couple celebrating their 50th wedding anniversary* （結婚50周年を迎えた夫婦）

A: This is the restaurant ¹(a. what b. where c. which) we celebrated our first wedding anniversary. And it's the same table ²(a. that b. who c. whose) we sat at, too.
B: But the waiter ³(a. that b. which c. who's) served us is different. Ha ha ha!

Good Reading

A 「失敗は成功のもと」に関する文章を読んで、下のa～cから適当な語句を選んで空所に書いてみましょう。その後で、音声を聞いて答えを確認しましょう。

Failure Leads to Success

In 1922, at the age of 20, Walt Disney started Laugh-O-gram Films. It was an animation studio [1]_____ supplied short silent films to movie theaters in Kansas City. However, Walt's unique and creative productions were expensive to make, and his business went bankrupt a year later. He spent his last dollars on a train ticket to Los Angeles. This was [2]_____ he created the little cartoon character named Mickey, [3]_____ went on to become the most famous character in animation history. Walt always said that his earlier failure with Laugh-O-gram was the reason [4]_____ he enjoyed later success.

Notes silent film「サイレント映画」 go bankrupt「破産（倒産）する」 cartoon「マンガ」

1. **a.** where **b.** which **c.** who
2. **a.** who **b.** why **c.** where
3. **a.** who **b.** whose **c.** when
4. **a.** when **b.** which **c.** why

B もう一度文章を読んで質問に最も合う選択肢を選びましょう。　CheckLink

1. Why did Laugh-O-gram Films fail?

Ⓐ The films were not popular.
Ⓑ The films cost a lot to produce.
Ⓒ The films were poorly made.
Ⓓ The films were not funny.

2. Where did Walt Disney create Mickey?

Ⓐ In Kansas City
Ⓑ On a train
Ⓒ In Los Angeles
Ⓓ In his childhood home

Writing—About Me

A Kaiの例を参考にして、今までで最高の授業について自分の情報を書いてみましょう。

About your best class ever...	Kai	You
What was the name of the class?	Advanced Mobile App Design	
When did you take the class?	senior year of university	
What was your school name and location?	CompTech University, Tokyo	
Who was the teacher?	Professor Ito	
Why did you like the class?	very practical, lots of one-on-one instruction	

Notes practical「実用的な」 instruction「指導」

B 下の関係詞を含む語句を使って、Kaiに関する文章を完成させましょう。

which is in Tokyo   *why I liked his class*   *who taught the class*
where I took it   *that I ever had*

The best class ¹_____ was called Advanced Mobile App
Design. I took it in my senior year of university. The name of the school
²_____ was CompTech University, ³_____.
Professor Ito was the teacher ⁴_____.
There are two reasons ⁵_____ : it was very
practical, and there was lots of one-on-one instruction.

C **B** を参考にして、自分のことを書いてみましょう。

The best class _____ was called _____.
I took it in _____. The name of the school
_____ is _____,
_____. _____
was the teacher _____. There are two reasons
_____ : _____
_____, and _____.

Word List

本書に登場する各Unitの重要語句を掲載してあります

Unit 1

p.12

airplane	名	飛行機
smooth	形	順調な
cabin attendant	名	客室乗務員
kind	形	親切な、やさしい
	名	種類

p.13

choice	名	選択
adjust	動	調節する
put on …		…を身に着ける
return	動 戻る 名 戻ること	
put up …		…を上げる
upright	形	まっすぐ立った、直立の
position	名	位置、職
Here you are.		はい、どうぞ
meal	名	食事

p.14

join	動	参加する
package tour	名	パック旅行
popular	形	人気のある
tourist	名	観光客
full of …		…でいっぱいの
departure	名	出発
museum	名	博物館、美術館
quiet	形	静かな
palace	名	宮殿
fasten	動	締める、留める
passport	名	パスポート

p.15

traveler	名	旅行者
economy class	名	エコノミークラス
group tour	名	団体旅行
take a picture		写真を撮る
suitcase	名	スーツケース
famous	形	有名な

stay	名	滞在、宿泊
	動	滞在する、宿泊する
airport	名	空港
duty-free	形	免税の
express train	名	急行列車
bad cold		ひどい風邪
clinic	名	診療所
hurry	動	急ぐ

p.16

major	形	主要な
million	形	百万の
excellent	形	優秀な、優れた
include	動	含む
educate	動	教育する

p.17

prefecture	名	県
location	名	場所
information technology	名	情報技術 (IT)
attend	動	出席する、通う
create	動	作る、創造する

Unit 2

p.18

host	名	主人、ホスト
	動	主人役として受け入れる、主催する
quickly	副	速く

p.19

parking lot	名	駐車場
office	名	会社、職場
hate	動	ひどく嫌う
crowded	形	混んでいる
sure	形	確信している
tired	形	疲れている
luggage	名	旅行カバン、手荷物

p.20

foreign	形	外国の
various	形	さまざまな
custom	名	習慣
make oneself at home		くつろぐ
introduce	動	紹介する、導入する

p.21

hobby	名	趣味
plate	名	皿
careful	形	注意深い、慎重な
burn	動	焼く、やけどさせる
recipe	名	レシピ
dish	名	料理、皿
bathroom	名	浴室、トイレ
gift	名	贈り物
help oneself to …		…を自由に食べる
favorite	形	大好きな、お気に入りの
actually	副	実際は
either	副	～も…でない
laundry room	名	洗濯室
feel free to …		自由に…する
washing machine	名	洗濯機

p.22

internship	名	インターンシップ、実務研修
hundreds of …		何百もの…
skill	名	技能、スキル
combine	動	組み合わせる
age	名	年齢
mealtime	名	食事の時間
fun	形	楽しい 名 楽しみ
activity	名	活動
advantage	名	よい点、メリット
time management	名	時間管理
safety	名	安全
opportunity	名	機会

p.23

height	名	身長、高さ
weight	名	体重、重さ
occupation	名	職業
terrible	形	ひどい、ひどく下手な、恐ろしい

Unit 3

p.24

wear	動	着る、身に着けている

p.25

lunch break	名	昼休み
ID badge	名	IDバッジ
office hours	名	就業時間、勤務時間
nearby	副	すぐ近くに
business casual		ビジネスカジュアル（カジュアルな仕事服）
dress code	名	ドレスコード、服装規定
meaning	名	意味
necessary	形	必要な
instead of …		…の代わりに
design department	名	デザイン部門

p.26

laptop	名	ノートパソコン
cabinet	名	キャビネット

p.27

closed	形	閉まっている
business hours	名	営業時間
meeting	名	会議、打ち合わせ
conference room	名	会議室
main entrance	名	正面玄関
report	名	報告書
take a break		休憩する
orientation	名	オリエンテーション、説明会
worker	名	労働者、社員

| information desk | 名 受付、案内所 |
| appointment | 名 予約、約束 |

p.28

access	名 入る権利
gym	名 体育館、ジム
cafeteria	名 食堂
organic garden	名 有機庭園
sports field	名 運動場
attraction	名 アトラクション、呼び物、名所
huge	形 巨大な
free	形 無料の
available	形 利用できる

p.29

| timetable | 名 時間割 |

Unit 4

p.30

| dessert | 名 デザート |
| delicious | 形 おいしい |

p.31

stomach	名 胃
hurt	動 痛む、傷つける
headache	名 頭痛
go for a walk	散歩に出かける
rest	名 休息、休養、残り
fantastic	形 素晴らしい、非常によい
especially	副 特に

p.33

reserve	動 予約する
cancel	動 キャンセルする、取り消す
sold out	売り切れる
far from ...	…から遠い

p.34

wet	形 濡れた
accident	名 事故
slide	動 滑る
line	名 路線
transportation system	名 交通機関
remain	動 …のままである、残る
mostly	副 主に、たいてい

p.35

| win | 動 勝つ |

Unit 5

p.36

shop	動 買い物をする
clothes	名 衣類、服
price	名 価格、値段
item	名 品物、商品、品目
successful	形 成功した

p.37

a couple of ...	2～3の…
cashier	名 レジ係
enough	形 十分な
wallet	名 財布

p.38

| furniture | 名 家具 |
| bread | 名 パン |

p.39

bakery	名 パン屋
cash	名 現金
medium	名 中間

p.40

patent	名 特許
durable	形 耐久性のある、丈夫な
perfect	形 完全な、申し分のない
workman	名 労働者

factory	名 工場
everywhere	副 どこでも
adult	名 大人
average	形 平均的な
own	動 所有する
be born	生まれる
purpose	名 目的
strength	名 強さ
unique	形 独特の、固有の
shape	名 形
fashionable	形 おしゃれな、流行している

p.41

cost	動 (お金が) かかる
	名 費用
second-hand	形 中古の
vintage	形 年代物の
tablet	名 タブレット
software	名 ソフトウェア

Unit 6

p.42

recently	副 最近
app	名 アプリ(applicationの略)
explain	動 説明する
whole	形 全体の
process	名 過程、一連の作業
work	動 (正しく) 機能する
useful	形 役に立つ、便利な
scary	形 恐ろしい、怖い
moment	名 瞬間、一瞬

p.43

manager	名 部長、マネージャー
visual	形 視覚の、目に見える
engineer	名 技術者、エンジニア
icon	名 アイコン、偶像
delete	動 削除する、取り除く

virtual	形 仮想の、事実上の
save	動 保存する、救う、節約する
amusement	名 娯楽、楽しみ
sound	動 …に聞こえる
tap	動 軽く叩く、タップする
scare	動 怖がらせる

p.44

responsible	形 責任がある
upgrade	動 高める、改善する
	名 改善、アップグレード
install	動 設置する、インストールする
mobile phone	名 携帯電話
switch	動 交換する、切り替える

p.45

browser	名 ブラウザ
streaming	名 ストリーミング
hack	動 不正侵入する
prefer	動 より好む
portable	形 携帯できる
GPS	名 全地球測位システム (Global Positioning Systemの略)
spell	動 つづる

p.46

appear	動 現れる
built-in	形 内蔵の
basic	形 基礎の、基本的な
developer	名 開発者
earn	動 稼ぐ
advertising	名 広告 形 広告の
within	前 …の中で、…以内に
provide	動 提供する、与える
later	副 後で 形 後の
spend	動 費やす、使う
character	名 登場人物、キャラクター

p.47

electrical	形	電気の
product	名	製品
refrigerator	名	冷蔵庫
freezer	名	冷凍庫
section	名	部分
allow	動	許す、許可する、可能にする
storage	名	貯蔵、保管
store	動	保管する、保存する
such as …		…など、…のような

Unit 7

p.48

paint	動	ペンキを塗る
	名	ペンキ
smoothly	副	順調に、スムーズに

p.49

checklist	名	確認リスト

p.50

repair	動	修理する
dig	動	掘る

p.51

heating system	名	暖房装置
replace	動	取り替える、交換する
gas	名	ガス
connection	名	接続
volunteer	名	ボランティア
	動	ボランティアする
pick up		拾う、拾い上げる
trash	名	ゴミ
fan	名	扇、扇風機
noise	名	騒音、雑音
garage	名	車庫、ガレージ
fix	動	修理する
tire	名	タイヤ

p.52

these days		この頃
clothing	名	衣類
original	形	独創的な
jewelry	名	宝石類
accessory	名	アクセサリー、装飾品
gain	動	手に入れる
personal	形	個人的な、個人の
satisfaction	名	満足（感）

p.53

maintenance	名	維持、保守、メンテナンス
cereal	名	シリアル
exercise	名	運動
sunscreen	名	日焼け止め
lift	動	持ち上げる
protect	動	保護する、守る

Unit 8

p.54

lie	動	横になる

p.55

cleanup	名	掃除、清掃
monthly	形	毎月の、月1回の
glad	形	うれしい
supplies	名	必需品、供給品
list	動	一覧表にする
slippery	形	滑りやすい

p.56

organic	形	有機栽培の、有機的な
ignore	動	無視する
global warming	名	地球温暖化
green	形	環境にやさしい
throw	動	投げる
garbage	名	（生）ゴミ
turn up …		…を上げる
heat	名	熱、温度

in the future	将来
environmentally	副 環境的に
friendly	形 友好的な、親切な、やさしい
air pollution	名 大気汚染

p.57

recycle	動 再利用する
environment	名 環境
electric	形 電気の、電気で動く
separate	動 分ける、分別する
reduce	動 減らす
law	名 法律
low-energy	形 低エネルギーの
light bulb	名 電球
plant	動 植える 名 植物
sign	名 看板、標識
	動 署名する
safe	形 安全な

p.58

lawyer	名 弁護士
overlook	動 見下ろす
entire	形 全体の、全部の
take action	行動を起こす
neighbor	名 隣人
over time	やがて、時間が経つにつれて
remove	動 取り除く、除去する
collect	動 集める、収集する

p.59

throw away	投げ捨てる、無駄にする

Unit 9

p.60

thanks to ...	…のおかげで
valuable	形 貴重な、価値のある
ability	名 能力
focus on ...	…に集中する

full-time	形 常勤の、正規の
ready	形 準備ができている

p.61

job fair	名 就職説明会
recruiter	名 採用担当者
hopefully	副 願わくは、できれば
job interview	名 就職面接
résumé	名 履歴書
completely	副 完全に

p.62

satisfied	形 満足した
work environment	名 労働環境
discuss	動 話し合う、議論する
matter	名 事柄、問題
	動 重要である
boss	名 上司
promotion	名 昇進
client	名 顧客

p.63

bonus	名 賞与、ボーナス
quit	動 辞める、退職する
retire	動 退職する
work overtime	残業する
hire	動 雇う
head office	名 本社
telework	名 在宅勤務

p.64

teleworking	名 在宅勤務
expert	名 専門家
predict	動 予測する
common	形 ありふれた、一般的な
disadvantage	名 不利な点、デメリット
employer	名 雇用主
electricity	名 電気、電力
commute	動 通勤する 名 通勤
lead to ...	…につながる
energy saving	名 省エネルギー

face-to-face	形 対面の 副 対面で
professional	形 職業上の
	名 専門家、プロ
social	形 社会の、社会的な
co-worker	名 同僚
isolated	形 孤立した
unmotivated	形 やる気のない
maximize	動 最大にする
minimize	動 最小にする
according to ...	…によると
salary	名 給料
customer	名 顧客
lack of ...	…の不足
direction	名 指示、方向
equipment	名 設備、機器

p.65

job title	名 仕事の肩書き、職名
yearly	形 その年の、年1回の
commuting time	名 通勤時間
achieve	動 成し遂げる、実現する

Unit 10

p.66

| passenger | 名 乗客 |
| educational | 形 ためになる |

p.67

tour conductor	名 添乗員
market researcher	名 市場調査員
research	動 調査する、研究する
check out ...	…を調査する
travel agency	名 旅行代理店
business card	名 名刺
on business	仕事で
expensive	形 値段が高い

p.68

| campaign | 名 キャンペーン |

competitor	名 競争相手、ライバル企業
profit	名 利益
marketing strategy	名 市場戦略

p.69

promote	動 宣伝する、促進する
advertise	動 宣伝する、広告する
loyal	形 忠実な
budget	名 予算
market share	名 市場シェア
word of mouth	名 口コミ
sales department	名 営業部
experienced	形 経験のある、経験豊富な
brochure	名 パンフレット
attractive	形 魅力的な
discount	名 値引き

p.70

translation	名 翻訳
belong to ...	…のものである
enter	動 入る、参入する
unfortunately	副 不幸なことに、あいにく
fortunately	副 幸運なことに、幸い
correct	動 訂正する、修正する
	形 正しい
buy up	買い占める
mistake	名 ミス、誤り

p.71

room rate	名 宿泊料金
atmosphere	名 雰囲気
pleasant	形 快適な、心地よい
convenient	形 便利な

Unit 11

p.72

| workplace | 名 職場 |

p.73

creativity	名	創造性
in fact		実際に
knowledge	名	知識
motivated	形	やる気のある
impressive	形	印象的な、素晴らしい
turn over		ひっくり返す、向きを変える

p.74

fill out		記入する
application form	名	申込用紙

p.75

personnel department	名	人事部
invitation	名	招待（状）
human resources	名	人材
application	名	応募、申込
schedule	動	予定に入れる

p.76

get ready for ...		…の準備をする
imagine	動	想像する
find out		見つける、発見する
double-check	動	再確認する、念を入れる
extra	形	余分な、追加の
applicant	名	応募者、申込者

p.77

inspire	動	刺激を与える、動機付ける
motivation	名	やる気、意欲、動機付け
motivate	動	やる気にさせる
inspiration	名	刺激（するもの）
importance	名	重要性

Unit 12

p.78

competitive	形	競争の激しい
harmful	形	有害な、害になる
society	名	社会

p.79

passion	名	情熱
positive thinking	名	前向きな考え方
fit	名 適合 動 適合する
support	動 支える、支援する
	名 支援、援助
afraid	形	怖がって、恐れて、心配して
hardly	副	ほとんど…ない

p.80

care	動	気にかける、気遣う
eco-friendly	形	環境にやさしい
point out		指摘する
scold	動	しかる
inexperienced	形	経験不足の、未経験の
work from home		自宅で働く
document	名	書類
improve	動	改善する
take over		引き継ぐ
work on ...		…に取り組む
paid leave	名	有給休暇
take place		行われる、開催される

p.81

alone	副	独りで
get along with ...		…とうまくやる
challenging	形	やりがいのある
fail	動	失敗する
supervisor	名	上司、監督者
fair	形	公平な
strict	形	厳しい、厳格な
expectation	名	期待
demand	名	要求

unrealistic	形	非現実的な
succeed	動	成功する
ambitious	形	野心的な、意欲的な
helpful	形	助けになる、頼りになる
fast-paced	形	ペースの速い
encouragement	名	励まし

p.82

basically	副	基本的に
personality	名	個性、性格
goal	名	目標、目的
likely	形	…しそうな
relationship	名	関係
productive	形	生産的な、生産性の高い
emphasize	動	強調する
make sure (that) …		…を確認する
describe	動	述べる、説明する
tradition	名	伝統
job hunter	名	求職者

p.83

outgoing	形	社交的な
shy	形	内気な
stubborn	形	頑固な
serious	形	まじめな、真剣な
immediate	形	すぐの、即座の
feedback	名	反応、意見

Unit 13

p.84

avoid	動	避ける
cause	動	引き起こす、原因となる
misunderstanding	名	誤解

p.85

ready-made	形	既製の、出来合いの
delivery	名	配達、配送

inbox	名	受信トレイ
mind	動	気にする、嫌がる
microwave	名	電子レンジ

p.86

follow	動	従う
keep in touch		連絡を取り合う
promise	動	約束する
reply	動	返信する　名 返信
as soon as possible		できるだけ早く
refuse	動	拒否する、断る
continue	動	続ける

p.87

urgent	形	緊急の
concern	名	心配事、懸念
expect	動	予期する、期待する
accounting	名	会計、経理
suggest	動	提案する、勧める

p.88

maintain	動	維持する
trusting	形	信頼できる
receiver	名	受信者
capital	形	大文字の
careless	形	不注意な
sender	名	送信者
attachment	名	添付書類

p.89

text	動	（携帯電話で）メールを送る
unknown	形	未知の

Unit 14

p.90

move	動	引っ越す　名 引っ越し

p.91

rent	名	家賃

greenery	名 緑の草木
lease	名 賃貸借（契約）
pack up	荷造りする

p.92

deliver	動 配達する

p.93

well-known	形 よく知られた、有名な
beginning	名 始まり、初め
damage	動 損害を与える、傷つける
earthquake	名 地震
furnish	動 備え付ける
agreement	名 合意、契約（書）
real estate agency	名 不動産代理店
architect	名 建築家
elderly	形 年配の
add	動 追加する、加える

p.94

resident	名 住人
in general	一般的に
utilities	名 公共料金
similar	形 同じような、似たような

p.95

residence	名 住居
ward	名 区
recommendation	名 おすすめ

Unit 15

p.96

request	動 依頼する、求める

p.97

graduate	動 卒業する
career	名 職業、経歴
get married	結婚する

pursue	動 追求する、追いかける
Congratulations	おめでとう
get sick	具合が悪くなる、病気になる
propose	動 提案する、結婚を申し込む

p.99

organize	動 組織する、運営する
contract	名 契約（書）
perform	動 演奏する、演じる、行う
business trip	名 出張
celebrate	動 祝う
anniversary	名 記念日
serve	動 給仕をする

p.100

failure	名 失敗
supply	動 供給する
creative	形 創造的な、独創的な
production	名 制作（物）
go bankrupt	破産（倒産）する
cartoon	名 マンガ
funny	形 おかしい、おかしな

p.101

advanced	形 上級の
senior	名 （高校・大学の）最終学年
practical	形 実用的な
instruction	名 指導

本書には CD（別売）があります

English Booster!

ストーリー＆必須文法で学ぶ
大学生の英語基礎力スタートアップ

2021 年 1 月 20 日　初版第 1 刷発行
2024 年 2 月 20 日　初版第 7 刷発行

著　者	Robert Hickling
	市　川　泰　弘
発行者	福　岡　正　人
発行所	株式会社　**金星堂**

（〒 101-0051）東京都千代田区神田神保町 3-21
Tel. (03) 3263-3828（営業部）
(03) 3263-3997（編集部）
Fax (03) 3263-0716
https://www.kinsei-do.co.jp

編集担当　今門貴浩　　　　　　　　　　Printed in Japan
印刷所・製本所／大日本印刷株式会社

ISBN978-4-7647-4113-3　C1082